The
Warren
Court

© Karsh of Ottawa 1964

The Warren Court

BY *John P. Frank*

PHOTOGRAPHS BY YOUSUF KARSH

The Macmillan Company
NEW YORK

TO

MY PARTNERS

IN THE PRACTICE OF

LAW

Contents

ix

Introduction

THIS BOOK is triply occasioned. A first motivation is my profound admiration for the photography of Yousuf Karsh, who seems to me to be the best now in this work. Second is a feeling that this Court is one of the most remarkable and significant the country has seen and that a contemporary impression, both photographic and verbal, is worth recording. Third, I had just finished writing the biography of a nineteenth century Justice and was dogged by the lack of a decent picture. If the country escapes atomic oblivion, many historians will be writing on these Justices a century from now, and for these brethren of the future, here is relief from the problem I have just faced.

This is not a book about either the Court or the law, except as the institution and its product necessarily intrude into individual accounts. I have said my best say on the Court in *Marble Palace,* published in 1958, and have written on the law in many places. There is as little about either here as possible in a necessarily interwoven field; the introductory chapter is intended to give only essential perspective, and the rest of the book is the Justices.

As for sources, in addition to books and articles, newspaper accounts, and decisions generally available, I have known most of these Justices for many years and have drawn freely on anecdotes or observations picked up in the course of time. There have also been interviews with many friends and associates of the Justices. I have felt two freedoms, one to draw on my own previous work with the uninhibited enthusiasm of a man for his favorite author, and the other to express opinions and make judgments. My work on the Supreme Court began twenty-five years ago, and I have reached some conclusions which are freely reflected.

While Mr. Karsh had done some of the Justices before, his own acquaintance with them and their personalities and their work has necessarily been limited. For his convenience in initially sizing up the Justices, I prepared a one-paragraph squib on each, and these are carried with the pictures. The paragraphs were to give him a starting point only; he spent several hours with each Justice, and the final conclusions as to proper portrayal are his.

My debts are many; I shall mention only three. Mr. Perry Knowlton, my agent at Curtis-Brown, Ltd., put this project together as a publishing venture. The costs of quality reproduction of photographs are high, and hence this was not an easy agent's job. His patience and interest have been extraordinary. Second, my wife and children have good-naturedly sacrificed a great deal of companionship by putting up with a lawyer-author in the house. Third, this book is dedicated to my partners. Having an author in the firm (for this is my fourth book in our ten years of partnership) is a little like keeping an elephant; it does become a burden. The secretarial services supplied, the cases handled by someone else in a deadline emergency, the drain on common income caused by a partner's pursuit of a not very lucrative hobby all create burdens for others. For their cheerful assumption, I am most grateful.

JOHN P. FRANK

Phoenix, Arizona
January, 1964

xii

Picture Notes

Pictures of the Chief Justice usually bring out the bland Scandinavian kindness and leave out the Viking. The Chief Justice is kind, he is wonderfully courteous, he is gentle in his dealings. But he is also prodigiously forceful, with locomotive drive. What he conceives to be constitutional wrong—segregation and restraints on free speech are examples—had best get out of the way before his train comes to the crossing. As a judicial administrator not simply for the Court but for the entire federal judicial system, he far outstrips all predecessors. He is the first true "Chief Justice of the United States," as distinguished from Chief Justice of the Supreme Court, the country has ever had. At the same time he puts his own personal stamp on his own judicial work. The task of the photographer is to suggest a personality which can be genuinely concerned with the meaningful lesser things—bankruptcy administration in New Hampshire or the operation of probation in North Dakota, for example—and at the same time take decisive hold of the ultimates of our society.

MR. JUSTICE HUGO L. BLACK

Justice Black is power and directness. His are the greatest successes of today's Court, and this is very probably because his is its least complicated personality. He has twin vitalities, an instinct for the jugular and an absolute dedication to the liberties of an American citizen. As the Black biography concludes, "His significance as a Justice is that he knows what to do with the power thus given him." He finds the point in a flash, and needs to spend very little time in self-torment over what to do about it. This extraordinary incisiveness is balanced by great gentleness and courtesy in his personal relations. Black truly thinks personal ill of no one. In more than twenty years at least, he has not been heard to express an ungenerous thought about a fellow human, and he probably does not have any. As the senior member of this Court, serving since 1937, he has had the rare triumph of beginning as one of a small minority and seeing many of his views on government and liberty become the law of the land. He has come to be generally regarded as one of the great Justices of the Court's history.

MR. JUSTICE WILLIAM O. DOUGLAS

Justice Douglas is the paradox of the Court because he mingles the opposites of directness and diversification. An old New Dealer, he is also a mountain climber, world traveler, a perennial best-selling author. He has a passion for the conservation of natural resources, not in some abstract or glorified way, but in terms of this mountainside or that stream. No eyes range as far as his from the Marble Palace in Washington across the hills and deserts of the world. Similarly on the Court his range is from the narrowly technical to the broadest stretch of policy, from tight analysis of an intricate corporate reorganization to basic issues of freedom. On all questions of human liberty, his is always the advance guard, and he has invariably been courageously outspoken even when the going was tough. A man who drives himself with extraordinary intensity and incredible speed, he has probably personally accomplished more in the past twenty-five years than any other two men in American public life. Douglas is the heritage of FDR's vigor.

MR. JUSTICE TOM C. CLARK

Justice Clark is the combination of Texas courtesy with Texas courage, the whole combined with constant application to duty. He is quick to decide; a lifetime around courthouses has given him the invaluable lesson that there is always another crisis around the corner, and we may as well get the current one, whatever it is, behind us now. More than any other Justice, he is the practitioner's judge, the Court member with the closest ties to bar groups because he is one of them. His bar connections are not for the collection of honorifics—he is a working bar member, not simply the recipient of awards and tributes to his station. All over America lawyers are practicing law differently, and usually a little better, because Clark is available as a counselor on hard, practical problems at their meetings or with their committees. He is also the champion of the career government lawyers, for he is the only man ever to work his way up through the ranks of the Department of Justice to Attorney General, and then to the Court. A Southerner, Clark has been an unshakably solid integrationist. He has also been a Court specialist on antitrust problems. As an occasional dissenter on the Court, he scores hard hits in a direct but gracious way. This is the hand of iron in the very velvet glove.

MR. JUSTICE JOHN MARSHALL HARLAN

Urbanity is the most conspicuous personal quality of Justice Harlan, temperateness and discriminating judgment his prime mental attributes. The only Justice to come to the Bench from a lifetime in a great Wall Street law office, he is the utter antithesis of the cartoon figure of a Big Business juggernaut. As a public figure, he regards himself as a trustee for the public interest, not a representative of any class; and so he brings an inquiring, questioning mind to his work. His convictions carry him into disagreement with his brethren rather more often than some of the other Justices. On such occasions his expressions are strong and clear but never unpleasant. It goes to the whole fiber of his character that he is a gracious man. He has a singularly objective approach to his work, an almost disembodied quality, as if Harlan the man were standing off watching Harlan the Justice search for the law. His is a mind which needs to know all the pros and cons, the details of the argument, before he makes up his mind; and then he is completely decisive.

MR. JUSTICE WILLIAM BRENNAN

If Justice Brennan has an enemy in the world, his name has escaped public record. Friendliness and kindliness are the most obvious attributes of this Justice. The most experienced of the nine as a judge before he came to the Supreme Court, Brennan has never become hardened in the work. Intellectually he is a Catholic humanist, broadly cultivated and in no way doctrinaire. His deepest commitment is to the values of individual freedom, and in all matters of speech, press, religion, or fair trial he searches the case and the Constitution to insure that the American traditions are fully respected. The process of his reasoning is likely to be intricate and detailed; this is no man for a quick thrust to a foreordained result. Patient, reasonable, extraordinarily thorough, he must satisfy himself, for he is a sort of Thomas Aquinas of the Court. His most remarkable attribute is that when the research is done, he repeatedly comes up with new ideas. The photographer's tough assignment is to suggest a man who is gaily good-natured and yet intensely earnest, one who totally exhausts the materials and yet never gets lost in them. A painstaking man, this, but with an easy humor.

MR. JUSTICE POTTER STEWART

Justice Stewart comes from a background of Ohio conservatism and carries with him that most astounding luggage, a free and inquiring mind. At first it was supposed that as a Justice he might be typed, falling into a readily predictable pattern. His first year on the Court blasted any such impression, and the years following buried it. Stewart on occasion stands alone; his views on the strict separation of church and state, for example, are not as strong as those of a majority of his brethren. His prose has wit without bite, charm without overstylishness. Because he avoids stereotype, he undertakes the burden of thinking for himself, freely contributing his own ideas and his own researches to the cases before him. As the first of the World War II generation to come to the Supreme Court, he is truly the modern man, and this reflects in every phase of his personality. Both quizzical and gracious, he represents an almost university style of investigation, usually reporting his results with blessed terseness. A man of strong convictions, he controls them with the spirit of fair-mindedness.

MR. JUSTICE BYRON R. WHITE

Justice White is the best possible exemplar for his administration President Kennedy could have chosen for the Supreme Court. No one could better represent the President's attitudes and spirit. White is a transplanted football player, Phi Beta Kappa, Rhodes Scholar, and eminently capable practicing lawyer; but all of this is of only passing, token importance in the post he now holds. Intellectually, White is the New Frontier at the height of its aspirations. Cool and dispassionate in judgment, technically able, White is a zealot neither for the judicial right nor the left. His is a mind fully capable of making practical judgments and close distinctions. A man of great personal reserve, he does not show his enthusiasms casually, and, unlike President Kennedy, his very real personal charm becomes apparent only gradually. His are a personality and ability which uniformly evoke quick respect and slower, but still uniform, affection. White's challenge to a photographer is that his so obvious competence could obscure every other phase of his personality—he is competent and he looks it. But his purely personal qualities have earned him the intense loyalty of everyone with whom he has worked closely. He is an ideal visitor for a university campus, where he can spend some hours with students; all will be his friends when he leaves.

x x

MR. JUSTICE ARTHUR GOLDBERG

This man bubbles, or sparks, or whatever other word can be chosen to describe a mind that turns out ideas as rapidly as the mint makes pennies. Justice Goldberg adheres firmly to the oldest of American values, but he has yet to be scared by a new idea. Traditions have force for him, but not habits. When the Metropolitan Opera was tied up by a strike, most Labor Secretaries would have regarded it as an unhappy but local problem, not up to Secretarial importance. Not the then Secretary Goldberg; he saw a national loss to music and he personally settled the strike. With his intellectual effervescence is combined a warm personality. Some of labor's representatives become hardened in the battles. The everlasting succession of emergencies, strain, and bitterness are souring experiences. But Goldberg is blessed not with a surface but a genuine, through and through, amiability; differences with him are problems, not passions. He makes decisions, not enemies. It is a fair bet that a large quota of the new legal thoughts from the 1960's to the 1980's will come from Goldberg. In the best and most constructive sense, his is a bright and engaging spirit.

The
Warren
Court

Chapter One

The Supreme Court

JUSTICE HOLMES once described the Supreme Court as quiet—with the quiet of a storm center. Seldom has the description been more appropriate than in the years of the Chief Justiceship of Earl Warren. Life in the Marble Palace has, as always, been quiet; but outside the winds of controversy have raged.

The Supreme Court is the one branch of American Government which can only take problems which come to it. The President and Congress, if so minded, can go hunting for trouble, passing laws, beginning investigations, issuing orders. The Supreme Court must wait for cases, actual lawsuits, to reach it. No case, no decision. But when the cases do come, they need decision. The past ten years have landed a bushel basket of tough ones on the Court's front steps.

If no case is ever brought on a particular subject, then the Court has nothing to do with that subject. The great problems of war and peace, of financial policy, including the general lines both of taxation and of appropriations, of national defense, and all the endlessly greater problems of international relations come before the Court scarcely at all. Because the Court can at most deal with problems of international relations only occasionally, it has a strong belief that it should leave them to the branches of the government which deal with them every day. For example, a leading 1964 decision in effect refused to decide whether Cuba's seizures of property were legal or not under international law. These problems of war and peace and revenue grow ever larger and may severely divide our citizens, but they rarely result in lawsuits and almost never present anything to the Court to decide.

Nevertheless, as has often been said, most great questions in America sooner or later do take the form of legal issues and so do reach the Supreme Court. Whether there could be a bank of the United States; whether ships or railroads may travel freely from state to state on the rivers or over the land of America; whether there could be slavery in the territories; whether a great business enterprise should exist—all these and countless other questions of national concern to Americans were presented to the Supreme Court in the form of cases before 1900.

During Chief Justice Warren's years of service since his appointment in 1953, an extraordinary number of important questions have come to the Court. It has had to decide:

1. Whether under the Constitution segregation could exist among American citizens.

2. Whether all Americans should have equal representation in Congress and state legislatures.

3. Whether states or school districts may require students to participate in religious exercises in the public schools.

4. How the fairness of American criminal trials can be improved by elimination of forced confessions; and whether everyone accused of a crime has a constitutional right to counsel to defend him.

5. Whether the laws provide means to preserve or re-create a free, competitive enterprise system in America.

6. What are the basic American rights of freedom of speech, press, and association and how they are to be protected and preserved.

7. Whether the administration of justice can be improved by rules of procedure and by superintendence of the operation of all federal courts.

In no decade of its history has the Court confronted more major questions than these. Happily, these questions have come before a Court of exceptional ability, what in history is called a "strong" Court. Like any institution, the Supreme Court, too, has its cycles, its moments of decline and of eminence. During the middle days of Chief Justice Marshall, from approximately 1810 to about 1829, the Supreme Court was probably the strongest, the most effective, the most significant branch of the national government. There were great legislative and executive moments as well—the Monroe Doctrine, for example, was announced in these years; but in that period John Marshall was the principal architect of the American Republic.

The next great period of Court eminence was in the last quarter of the nineteenth century. These are the years of the almost faceless Presidents, the men who sink in bearded anonymity into America's political past. In those years a divided Congress served briefly and, with a few spectacular exceptions, did little. The Supreme Court of the United States was at the peak of its powers and talents. At no time in American history have we ever had so completely dominating a Court as this of the late nineteenth century, a Court overshadowing the whole remainder of the Government. Its dominance is illustrated in an eminent American historian's collection of the key documents of American history. For the period between the death of Marshall in 1835 and the inauguration of President Lincoln in 1861, the volume includes approximately fifty documents of which about 5 per cent are United States Supreme Court decisions. The same collection for the years 1871 to 1898 (the eve of the Spanish-American War) prints about seventy documents, a full 25 per cent of them United States Supreme Court decisions.

The Court was exceptionally capable, and exercised remarkable influence in American life during the 1920's and early 1930's, when this Court under Chief Justice Hughes finally collided flatly with the program of the New Deal and President Roosevelt. That controversy receded after 1937 as new personnel came to the Court. By 1951 the Court had slid to the point of apathy.

In an article I wrote in 1951 I described the Court as "an institution of dwindling significance in American life." The name of that article was "The Court and the Constitution: the Passive Period," and in retrospect, the title was about right. But, as the same article noted, "there is power latent in passivity." If, in 1850 (the article concluded), "a commentator had predicted that the Court and the

3

Constitution had no important future in American life, he would have been reasonable; but he would have been wrong." For some of the greatest days of the Court still lay ahead of it.

The passive period ended with the appointment of Chief Justice Earl Warren by President Eisenhower in 1953. The appointment as Chief of one of the most dynamic and vital figures in American public life began bringing the process of the Court to a level of effectiveness which would enable it to meet the great problems lying ahead. The subsequent appointments by both President Eisenhower and President Kennedy of a series of four very able Associate Justices still serving has completed the revival of the Court. The same decade has seen Congress in one of its periods of lag, with the House of Representatives in particular having wandered into procedural byways which has made it almost impossible for that body to function at all. The general impasse between Presidents and Congress has gone far to neutralize the effectiveness of either of those branches. The practical result has shown that not only has there been a strong Court, but that it has looked disproportionately important because at times in the past decade it has been almost the only instrument of government capable of functioning.

No Court with big decisions to make has ever been popular with everyone, and the Warren Court has been no exception. A decision would not be "big" if there were not some division among our people on the issue. Losers are usually disappointed; some are bitter.

Our own day is no exception. The wildest critics have been the John Birch Society, who want to remove the Chief Justice. Perhaps the most specialized group in America is the Arizona Mothers to Impeach Earl Warren. Apart from the lunatic fringe, the most passionate critics break into three groups.

1. *The Segregationists.* The Court has, with a relentless and unmistakable voice, held over and over again that all Americans must have equal treatment, and that no government can discriminate among

4

its citizens on the basis of their color. The decisions of the past ten years have climaxed an unmistakable trend begun almost fifty years ago.

These decisions do go against the grain for many citizens, and their enforcement has resulted in the greatest civil strife in the United States since Lincoln's day. Inevitably, those dissatisfied with the results are outspokenly bitter against the Court.

2. *Those who stand to lose power under the redistricting cases.* American democratic government assumes that in the national House of Representatives and in at least one house of the state legislatures, people will be represented substantially equally. If this is to be so, the election districts must each have about the same population. Yet many Congressional districts or state legislatures have not been revised to keep up with the population shift from country to town, so that in many places there are ten times more voters in one district than in another.

The Supreme Court has held that each American vote should count the same. When the Court made these decisions concerning representation in Congress and concerning one house of the state legislatures, a Constitutional amendment was proposed to reverse these decisions. While these decisions have been violently attacked, they have also been warmly praised. Most Americans have regarded the decisions as to the national Congress and the one house of the state legislatures as the beginning of a long-overdue reform. The amendment started with a rush and was endorsed by a dozen state legislatures but finally slowed to a halt.

In June of 1964 the Court made new law by extending this same principle to the other house of the state legislatures. This new move may revive the proposal for a Constitutional amendment.

3. *Those genuinely concerned about religion.* The Court's race-relation decisions have been intensely controversial in one region, and the redistricting cases have been unpopular among special groups

5

which will lose power by them. The most generally controversial decisions of all have been those on religion in education. These had their hot attackers and strong supporters in every part of the country.

In America, education is free to the consumer, if costly to the taxpayer; it is also compulsory. This much is clear. The great question has been whether it should also in some manner be religious.

The question comes up in many ways. Can religious teaching be carried on in the schools during school hours? Can the students be required to recite either some nondescript prayer composed for them by someone in the state's education department, or some great classic like the Lord's Prayer? Shall such prayers be said in the schools at all? And—always at the root of the matter—can tax money be appropriated for religious education?

The Court had taken its answer from the first provision of our Bill of Rights which bars "the establishment of religion" or interference with its "free exercise." Fully recognizing that ours is dominantly a religious people, the Court has also recognized that ours is the religion of diversity. Whose religion shall be taught? Which bible read? Which version of the Lord's Prayer recited? Moreover, some of our people are nonbelievers, and their rights must be respected, too.

Hence the Court has held that the taxpayers may not be taxed and children compelled to attend school to promote any religious activity. Our doctrine of separation of church and state means that prayers are the proper business of every man's home, Sunday school, or church; it is his business, not the state's.

A key decision in this series aroused a tremendous storm. The Court was violently denounced as antireligious from coast to coast. A constitutional amendment was proposed to reverse the decision.

Rarely has a major storm blown up so quickly or subsided so rapidly. Catholic, Jewish, and Protestant justices had agreed on this school prayer issue. As the problem began to be fully understood, many churches themselves lined up with the Court. It was quickly realized that any prayer so "neutral" as to please all our many faiths would be meaningless and empty. A new recognition of the value of separation of church and state followed. When a second separation case was decided a year after the controversial decision, it was accepted without serious murmur. Consideration of a constitutional amendment to alter the result is proceeding very slowly.

Attacks on the Court have been frequent since Washington's day, and they always keep the same old flavor. To the critics of 1821 it appeared that the liberties of America were being annihilated by the Court. Chief Justice Marshall was attacked by the Chief Justice of Virginia for what the state judge regarded as his "monstrous" conduct, for decisions by Marshall which could only be the product of "that love of power which all history informs us infects and corrupts all who possess it," for reaching for the "zenith of despotic power." Another Marshall critic described one of his decisions as dealing a "death blow . . . at the very existence of the states," and went on to say that Marshall's decisions were working a "revolution" and were destroying "that Constitution which our fathers have given us."

As for impeachment, Theodore Roosevelt thought this much too slow and fuddy-duddy a method of dealing with the Court. He believed that decisions should be recalled by popular vote and that judges should be removed by simple majorities of Congress when they were, as he saw it, out of touch with the times.

Meanwhile, the Court keeps doing its business unflustered at the same old stand. Warren has made the most of his position, as did John Marshall a century and a half ago, because he happens personally to have extraordinary leadership capacities; but this is a factor of the man, not of the position of the Chief Justice. The "Warren Court" is an assembly of nine men who as individuals and as a group, by comparison with their historic predecessors, have an extraordinarily high level of ability. The great Marshall Court had among its members the Chief Justice himself and two able associates; but the rest of his group was largely an aggregation of ciphers. Such Marshall side Justices as Henry Brockholst Livingston or Gabriel Duval are not only unknown today;

7

they were of no significance or stature in their own day either. The Court of Chief Justice Taft was extraordinarily capable, having between 1925 and 1930 not only the Chief Justice, but also Justice Holmes, Justice Brandeis, Justice Sutherland, and Justice Stone. Each, in his very different way, was immensely capable. But that Court also had several other Justices of no more than minimal accomplishments.

Each President in choosing a Supreme Court Justice makes the best choice he can. All he can do is study the record of the man he appoints, and hope. The appointment is for life. Some of them are bound to be more successful than others. There have been about one hundred Justices since Washington's time, and inevitably a small number have been utterly incompetent or wildly eccentric. Some have been great. Happily, the heavy majority have been at least adequate.

Probably the ablest Court which ever sat was that of 1880. Its very capable Chief Justice was Morrison R. Waite. Its ablest associates were Justices Field, Miller, and Bradley, and at the very next line of ability were Justices Harlan and Strong. Its weaker members were Justices Swayne, Clifford, and Woods, the latter two approaching the negligible in terms of any substantial contribution to the law.

For the plain ability of its members, the Warren Court, as it has come to exist, compares favorably with any Court in American history, including the Court of 1880. Some of the particulars as to each Justice are contained in this volume. Since 1800, each President choosing a Chief Justice has used even greater caution than in his other appointments so that most of the Chiefs have been among the outstanding public servants of their generations. Of Chief Justices Marshall, Taney, Waite, Taft, Hughes, and Stone, this is most assuredly true; and from every standpoint of administration, ability, and output Chief Justice Warren belongs in that great tradition.

Of the Associate Justices, Justice Black is the senior, having been on the Court since 1937. He would surely be on anyone's list of the ten outstanding, and most influential Justices in the history of the Court. His driving force, eloquence, brevity, and capacity for plain hard work have left their mark on every phase of the Court's jurisdiction. Similarly effective has been William O. Douglas, the one Justice who is so quick that a full-time judicial assignment can keep him only half busy. His twentieth book recently came off the press, all written since he has been on the Court.

The appointments of Justices Black and Douglas date back to the 1930's. More than ten years their junior is Justice Tom Clark, appointed to the Court by President Harry Truman. Clark, rather to the surprise of many who underestimated him at the time of his appointment, has proved to be one of the most effective of the Justices. In a half-dozen major fields of judicial accomplishment during the Warren years, leading opinions are his; and his work for the improvement of the administration of justice by the various state court systems is more ambitious than any Justice has ever before attempted.

The three Eisenhower appointees to this Court are Justices John Harlan, William Brennan, and Potter Stewart. Justice Harlan, who came to the Court from a short experience on a Court of Appeals and who previously had been a member of one of the great law firms of America, has without exception turned out opinions of polish, elegance, and skill. Justice Brennan, who combines the amiable good nature of an Irish politician (which he was not) with the sheer hard labor of a railroad section hand on a hot day (which he also was not), has been an immense blessing to the Court. His scrupulous searching out and consideration of detail help others to avoid error and make for a more precise Court product. Justice Stewart, also a former Court of Appeals judge, is a completely careful craftsman who combines a bright insight with complete understanding of subject matter and an altogether pleasing capacity to turn a phrase.

The two junior Justices are the Kennedy appointees, Justices Byron White and Arthur Goldberg. Both have served too briefly for an opinion concerning them to be more than an informed hunch. On the basis of that hunch, and of careful consideration of all of their work, they should prove to be two of the most capable Justices of this

9

century. They are very different, each an admirable complement for the other. White has a meticulousness with genuinely important detail somewhat greater than Goldberg's; the facts which may affect the consequence will never slip through his net. On the other hand, Goldberg is a little more provocative, the more likely of the two to spark off an entirely new line of thought. The judicial output of each can safely be expected to be thoroughly satisfactory from the standpoint of skill and effort.

These nine Justices are very different one from another. Except for the fact that all are lawyers, are native born, were in military service, and are proved hard workers, they have very little personally in common. They come from the East, Midwest and West, North, and South. As practicing lawyers, some represented business, some labor. Six are Democrats, three Republicans. Some were nationally known at the time of their appointments, some generally unknown. They are all law-school graduates, and three had training at English universities.

As for the Justices, what do they do? What is the job which the American people have assigned to this part of its government?

The Supreme Court of the United States is the highest Court of the land for both the state and the federal systems, but its duties in respect to the two are very different. On the cases which begin in the state courts, only those which turn on the interpretation of the United States Constitution, or an Act of Congress, or a treaty, can ever rise from a state court to the Supreme Court; for all the rest, the state supreme court is the end of the road. This means that 99 per cent of the state cases must stay in the state courts. Any normal or routine will contest, or auto accident, or quarrel over a contract presents no issue which has any federal connection at all. No one has ever counted all the state cases filed each year; a guess is about two and one half million. Only 1 per cent of these, or less, can even theoretically reach the Supreme Court. Of the cases which begin in the federal courts, theoretically all of them can be reviewed by the Supreme Court, but this is only theoretical. There are so many thousands of cases in the federal courts each year that the Supreme Court would be hopelessly swamped if it attempted to look at more than a few of them. To prevent this overloading, Congress has given the Court the power to decide what cases it will hear.

In the most recent year for which statistics are available, there were almost 250,000 civil, criminal, and bankruptcy matters begun in the district courts. If we assume 2,500,000 state matters, the total is 2,750,000 legal starts. Meanwhile about 900 appeals went to the Supreme Court from all courts, state and federal, plus about 1,000 special criminal matters which we may ignore because they take very little time of the Court. The percentage then, of all legal matters begun in America which never reach the Supreme Court is over 99.99 per cent.

But the thousand or so cases which are brought to the Court are not necessarily accepted by it. Most of the cases are presented on petitions to be heard, known as petitions for certiorari. The nine Justices could not possibly decide a thousand cases a year with opinions. If this many cases were actually argued for an hour on each side, it would take fifty forty-hour weeks just to listen to them, without any time for research and writing. As a practical matter, therefore, the Court usually hears between 10 and 15 per cent of the appeals presented to it, with a net number of opinions in well under 150 cases a year.

What kind of cases come to the Court? In any given year around 30 per cent have to do generally with the problems of business, with the economic system of the country. This includes the interpretation of the Acts of Congress regulating business, such as the labor laws or Federal Trade Commission Act, or the securities Acts. It includes the antitrust cases, and transportation cases concerning the regulations of railroads, airlines, and motor carriers, and occasionally shipping cases as well. Closely related are the interpretations of what the tax laws mean.

Roughly another third of the business goes to matters of jurisdiction and procedure and matters of relationships between the federal government and the states. The Supreme Court makes rules for the court system of the United States and determines what cases may be heard in the federal courts and how they shall be tried. The federal-state cases may involve the operations of the other, or how much a state may regulate or tax the interstate commerce which comes across its borders.

The final third of the cases, in addition to a few purely criminal matters, are those which involve some claimed interference with the constitutional liberty of an American citizen. Prior to 1925, the Supreme Court usually reviewed such matters only if the claimed abuse was by the federal government. Since 1925, when it expanded its jurisdiction, the Court has supervised both state and federal justice, both state and federal claimed interferences with individual freedom. The cases involving freedom of speech and press, freedom of religion, fair trial, searches and seizures, voting rights, and race relations are what are commonly called "civil liberties cases."

This, then, is the business of the Supreme Court of the United States: the business of business itself, the business of taxation, the business of criminal law, the business of proper court practice, the business of the relation of the states to each other and to the federal government, the business of the rights of an American citizen.

If one is to understand the role of the Supreme Court in American life, one's mind must never wander far from the question of quantity. One must never forget that there will only be from 100 to 150 opinions coming from the Supreme Court each year. If, for example, in any given year the Supreme Court determined to devote itself altogether to supervising criminal practice, and if there were 25,000 criminal cases filed in the United States in that year, the most the Supreme Court could possibly write on would be 150; of sheer necessity, 24,850 cases could never be decided by that Court.

Thus there are two vital elements if the Court is to be effective. First, it must stick to the big questions. The little ones will have to be decided by someone else. Second, the Court performs its function by leadership, by laying out general principles and giving an example for the lower courts to follow. It is like the quarterback on a football team. It puts the play in motion, it throws the ball, but unless there is some-one at the other end to catch that pass, and run with it, no actual headway is going to be made. This is vividly true, for example, in the race-relations field. When in 1954 the Court declared that school segregation was unconstitutional, President Eisenhower caught his pass and proceeded forthwith to direct an end to school segregation in the District of Columbia. Because his staff and persons under his direc-tion carried out his command, segregation was ended in the District of Columbia. On the other hand, in that school district in South Carolina which primarily triggered the segregation cases in the first place, there was no one waiting with any particular enthusiasm to carry out the Supreme Court's opinions; and the practical result is that all of the children originally in that case who originally won that "victory" have passed through the grade schools and the high schools without ever coming into an unsegregated school at all. The Court must do most of its deeds by a combination of inspiration, direction, and teaching.

As the country expands, there is an inevitable question as to the future of the Supreme Court in American life. America's population has passed from 120,000,000 to 180,000,000 in thirty years; it will doubtless be up to a quarter of a billion by some time in the foreseeable future if nuclear warfare does not decimate us. Fifty million extra people have extra problems, and the problems of the whole country will grow more and more difficult with an expanding population. The Congress has tried to keep pace with growth by vastly expanding its staff and by staying in virtually permanent session. The Presidency and the Executive Department have expanded tremendously, so much so that the President's personal entourage, described by the gener-alized name, "the White House," is now more descriptive of a personnel army than of a place of abode. Yet the Supreme Court con-tinues to consist of nine Justices as it has for almost a hundred years; the only significant personnel additions are a few secretaries and a very small number of law clerks. Can this little institution keep pace with the needs of America, and if so, how?

The Court has at least three devices available for keeping pace with the rising tide of Americans without any conflict with its basic traditions of careful workmanship and mature judgment:

First, the Court has in the past solved the problem of keeping pace by dropping certain types of cases from its consideration. For example, the Court in prior decades decided many cases which had no greater claim upon its attention than that the case arose between citizens of different states. With the passing of the years these cases have been dropped almost altogether. On the docket of the present Court the list of cases presently decided is by no means a constant parade of great antitrust cases or great civil rights issues or great anything else. There is still a fair number of relatively minor matters on the Supreme Court docket which could go if more serious business pressed. Justices Harlan and Stewart, in particular, feel that one class of cases to which the Court has given some attention, the matter of the details of jury trials in personal injury cases, could well go off the docket. Other Justices regard these as involving important matters in the preservation of the constitutional right of jury trial. But whether these be regarded as important or not, not more than about half of all the cases are of a high degree of public importance. There is a little slack in the docket.

Second, the Court can when it must somewhat increase its own efficiency. Styles in judicial opinions change like other styles. For the past twenty years, opinions have been growing longer; and separate or individual opinions and dissents have become more frequent. While the Warren Court of today turns out very substantially more work than the rock bottom reached shortly before Warren came to the Court, the total number of cases actually decided by opinion is far less than it was in the 1920's and 1930's. Many today look longingly back to those terser and less individualistic eras at a style whose return would be most welcome. Here too is a slack which can be taken up when it needs to be. Justices Black and Douglas, veterans of those earlier days, proved then that they could easily turn out far more opinions than they are called upon to produce today. Chief Justice Earl Warren, in whose administration output has increased, is confident that output could be greatly increased again if there were need to do so; and Justice Clark holds in reserve a belief that the Court might if necessary hear more cases by the simple expedient of sitting longer each day.

Third, the Court has learned to increase its effectiveness as a national leader both by a kind of administration and a kind of legislation. Administration is left largely to the Chief Justice. Chief Justice Warren meets regularly with the lower-court judges of the country and, through an administrative office which he directs, very substantially affects the operations of the whole federal court system. On the legislative side, Congress has given to the Court the power to make rules of procedure and there are whole battalions of committees of lawyers, scholars, and judges at work in constant studies to keep the legal system in tune with the needs of the times. In John Marshall's day, such matters had to be decided a case at a time; now the rule-making process may govern untold numbers of cases without deeply involving the Court's time at all.

The result is that for the foreseeable future, the Court should be able to do its job. That it is having substantial effect on American life during the Warren years is apparent to every citizen. The Court has set its hand to the plow of desegregation, and real though slow progress is being made in desegregation. The Court has declared for the general principle of equality in election districts, and election districts are being made more equal. To pick one tangible, dollar item, the Court directed that Du Pont should be severed from General Motors, and Du Pont has been selling its General Motors stock. The Court in the Chief Justiceship of Earl Warren has had a real impact.

While the Warren Court has assuredly been more active than its passive predecessor and has occupied a far larger role on the American scene, it, like its predecessor, has always been true to the historic role

15

of the Court. It has been one of the genuine glories of American history that the Court has ever been a place to which come men, usually able and almost always dedicated, to gather to deliberate on fundamental problems of the American people. One may not always be satisfied with the result, whatever it may be, and still be grateful for the existence of the process itself. The fundamental triumph of the Court has been the integrity of that process and the patriotism of its members. Anyone of independent point of view is certain to find what he regards as error in some portions of the Court's work, but he will find little that is ignoble. It is for this reason that while the Court may often be subject to purely partisan attack, it is always regrettable when this is so. From John Marshall to Earl Warren, those who have mounted the Bench have given their best to the service of their country.

Chapter Two

CHIEF JUSTICE
Earl Warren

IN CHIEF JUSTICE WARREN'S first year on the Supreme Court a little ceremony was repeated for 1,567 lawyers admitted to Supreme Court practice. Each newcomer stepped before the Court. As his name was called, some already established bar member moved the admission of the new man. Warren paused, called the man by name, and gave him the famous Warren smile of welcome.

Time passed. Ten years later, an observant person paid a first visit to the Supreme Court chamber. Warren was ten years older, and by this time the number of lawyers who had been admitted was not 1,500, but 15,000. When the new lawyers were being admitted, each with Warren's flash of cordiality, the observer was heard to whisper, "He actually makes each one feel personally welcome!"

This little courtesy was unnecessary. The lawyers could be admitted in the clerk's office without taking Court time at all. Even with the traditional open Court ceremony, they could certainly be admitted without the Chief taking time to address each one—a nod of the head would do it. Yet after ten years Warren was treating each person as individually as when he began.

But there was a difference. When Warren came to the Bench, each new lawyer was admitted upon a statement by his sponsor that "I have examined his credentials in the office of the Clerk and am satisfied that he possesses the necessary qualifications." Ten years later the little sentence had been shortened; it was obviously immaterial where the sponsor had seen the credentials, and all he said was "I am satisfied that he possesses the necessary qualifications." The thirteen eliminated words, if said in a dignified way, take about four seconds. Four seconds repeated a thousand times (sometimes several lawyers are admitted together), is four thousand seconds, sixty-six minutes, a little over an hour. The Court could save that hour of time, could put it to more constructive use. The cordial greeting, the hour saved—these are two sides of the Warren personality. He wants the judicial machine to run as swiftly and efficiently as possible, but never at the expense of the individual.

The Chief Justiceship of the United States is, beyond most offices, what its holder makes of it. The Constitution makes no special provision for the Chief Justice; the only reference to him is that in the case of a trial for the impeachment of the President, the Chief Justice shall preside; happily, this has occurred only once in American history. George Washington's Congress of 1789 created the Court providing for "a Chief Justice and five associate Justices" as the number then was. The title of the position as "Chief Justice of the United States" was stabilized by law in the year 1866 and has continued. What the wearer of the title does is a mixture of tradition and the personality of the particular Chief Justice. His two most important special functions are first, that he is Chairman of the conferences of the Court, and so leads the discussion when the Justices gather together each week to decide their cases. Second, he assigns the writing of the opinions, for while each Justice may, if he wishes, write on every case, the practice since John Marshall's time in 1801 has been to strive for one opinion of the Court. If the Chief himself is in the majority, it is up to him to choose who shall write.

Warren has put a whole new dimension on the job. He came to the Court after ten years of experience as Governor of California, which was then on its way to being what it has since become, the nation's largest state. The administrative problems of a Governor of California are prodigious; it is one of the greatest executive jobs in America. The Governor is responsible for the performance of thousands upon thousands of employees engaged in hundreds of projects, for the making of great budgets, for leading the legislature, for an endless number of appointments.

As Chief Justice, Warren is the administrative head of the Supreme Court, but giving him the traditional or obvious administrative duties is a little like giving the head of America's largest bank a child's savings account to manage; it is not likely to take him very long. Superintending the few employees of the Supreme Court building, having the reports properly published, seeing to it that the clerk's office keeps proper track of the cases—such chores if put into the hands of an able staff, cannot occupy Warren much.

Warren, therefore, has taken over ultimate responsibility for the management of the judicial system of the United States. In days now gone, the management of the work of the federal courts around the country was no one's responsibility. Each district judge was a local lord responsible for his own domain. If he got the job done, good. If he did not, the people of that state could simply endure it and wait for the next judge to be appointed. If conditions became too bad, perhaps because of expanding population, the state might hope for an Act of Congress under which a new judge could be appointed. But there was no central management of this system at all.

This condition began to change in 1922 when William Howard Taft was Chief Justice and obtained the passage of an act for the creation of a Judicial Conference of the United States. Under his leadership, this was a gathering of the senior federal appeals judges from each region of the country. The Conference came in time to be an old gentlemen's club, pleasant but giving very little actual leadership.

Succeeding Chief Justices have attempted to make more of the Conference, but it remained for Warren really to take hold. What followed was a quiet revolution. When Warren became Chief, the members of the Judicial Conference averaged about eighty years of age, and the Chief Justice, while he presided over their discussions, did not vote. Warren changed all this. He quietly saw to it that when a judge became seventy he would no longer be in charge of administration in his circuit nor represent it at the Conference. Warren himself is seventy-three, but he recognizes that, on the average, few judges can carry administration after this age. Instead, that responsibility passes to a younger man.

The next step, after cutting down the average age of the Conference, was to bring in the trial judges. Up to this time, the Judicial Conference had consisted of the senior judges of the eleven appeals courts which cover the United States. These appeals judges believed that they could reflect the views of the trial judges of their own regions. Warren doubted that this was so, but he prefers to lead gently where he can, so he simply suggested that the trial judges be asked whether they felt that the appeals judges adequately represented them. Upon a poll, 75 per cent of the trial judges declared that they would prefer to speak for themselves. Warren then brought them in.

Having made the group younger and broadened its base, it remained to furnish leadership. It seemed to Warren that if the Chief was to be a participant, he should really participate, and so he does, voting along with the others.

Having thus created a workable institution of young and vigorous men, it remained to give them plenty of good solid work to do; and this Warren has also done. All legislation concerning the federal courts is likely either to start with the Conference or be referred to it for check. All rules for all federal courts are basically the responsibility of the Conference. The local divisions of the Conference have the responsibility of managing affairs in their own areas.

At the same time Warren took charge of the Administrative Office of the federal courts. With an exceptionally able man of his own choosing as Director and a valuable second-in-command for the important statistical work of the office, Warren began personally to direct the operation of the federal court system. If one region of the country now falls behind in its work because of a sudden burst of new cases or because a judge is ill, the Administrative Office will find someone to help carry the load. If any particular judge is failing to carry his load, his record will look very bad in the annual statistical reports. The federal district judges remain powerful and useful figures in their states; their independence is fiercely preserved. But the days of the local tyrant whose whim could victimize a region are now largely gone.

Warren's final instrument to improve the federal court system has been by rule making. In the 1930's the detail was too great for Congress, which gave the Supreme Court power to make rules for the federal courts. These rules are laws governing how the courts shall work, laws that are made by the Supreme Court itself rather than Congress. The rules cover countless matters—who can be included in a lawsuit, what questions each side has to answer for the other before the trial begins, how some matters are to be presented to the judge for his decision and others to the jury for its holding, and so on. These rules matters involve not hundreds but thousands of details. The two standard texts on only one portion of the rules run seven fat volumes apiece.

Rule making flourished for a time, but after 1949 it ground to a total halt. One of Warren's first problems was to get rule making off the ground and working again. After meeting with the Judicial Conference, he finally led the way to a whole new system, had six separate committees appointed to do rules work, and now has the machinery at full blast. Warren personally is the heart and soul of what makes these committees go. He selects their membership with great care, drawing on lawyers, judges, and law professors around the country; one of the most hardworking committees, for example, is headed by Mr. Dean Acheson, who is head of a great law firm as well as former Secretary of State and who himself works as hard at his committee duties as any other member. Warren personally meets for at least some of the time with each committee, giving the closest possible attention to its work and sometimes joining in its discussion. The committees, not unnaturally, take the view that if what they are doing is worth the bother of the Chief Justice of the United States it is worth renewed effort on their part, and they buckle into their jobs a little harder than before. The committee reports then go to the Judicial Conference, to the Supreme Court, and finally to Congress with Warren personally guiding each step of the way.

This does not mean that Warren is personally actually doing what the Conference, committees, and staff get done. He is a dedicated believer in delegation of responsibility on the Supreme Court just as he was as Governor. The Director of the Federal Courts, for example, comes from his office in the Supreme Court building to bring his problems in to the Chief, receives some general guidance, and then tends to the details himself. But Warren realizes completely that the Chief must participate and must take the lead if the system is to work successfully. If he chooses able subordinates, he can expect others to follow once he shows the way.

The result is that Warren is the first true "Chief Justice of the United States," as distinguished from being the "Chief Justice of the Supreme Court," that the country has ever had. There have been prodigiously able men in the office of the past; the Chief Justiceship has earned the greatest tradition of ability of any office in American life ever since the days of John Marshall. But no one has ever taken hold of the entire system in this manner before.

In no place is Warren's personal hold on the court system more clearly shown than at the annual meeting of the American Law Institute. This is an organization of some 1,500 lawyers and judges from about the country which meets annually in Washington to consider matters of concern in the legal systems of all courts of the country, state and federal. The Chief Justice regularly attends these meetings and makes an annual report of his own. When in attendance, he follows the discussion with the extraordinary attention of an intense listener, following each speaker with his eyes and his ears, attention completely focused. When he makes his own report, what is remarkable is not his planned speech, because doubtless the administrative office supplies paragraphs which could be presented by anybody. What is more impressive than the planned remarks are the spontaneous comments and observations he makes as he goes along. The topics in his planned text bring his mind to other related illustrations, and so he spontaneously speaks of problems of improving the probation system of one area of the country or of bringing down the costs of bankruptcy administration in another. As one listens, the realization washes over the audience that the legal system of the United States is not simply a headless juggernaut; there is one single individual in authority who actually knows what is going on from coast to coast and is concerned about making it go better.

Warren's name is Americanized from his ancestral Norwegian; his grandfather was Halvar Varran. His father was a railroad mechanic. He was himself born in Los Angeles on March 19, 1891, and attended the University of California from which he received his basic college and law degrees in 1912 and 1914. From 1914 to 1917 he practiced law in the San Francisco area. In 1917 and 1918 he was in the Army, finishing as a first lieutenant in the infantry.

From the end of World War I until the present, Warren has been active in public life. He was a city and county prosecuting attorney from 1919 to 1939, serving as district attorney for Alameda County from 1925 to 1939. For the next four years he was Attorney General of California. Then, in 1943, Warren hit the big time. He became Governor of California and continued in that office until he went to the Supreme Court ten years later.

The migration to the American West, and particularly to California, after World War II has been the largest movement of people in the history of the United States and one of the largest mass migrations in the history of the world. Between 1940 and 1960, the population of California increased from about 7,000,000 to about 16,000,000. An increase of this magnitude is not simply growth, it is an explosion, and Warren was in the Governor's chair just in time to pick up the pieces. The community responsibilities in terms of schools, water supply, public health, law enforcement, roads, and in terms of the taxes necessary to pay for it all created prodigious burdens which Warren met with skill, good humor, and poise.

Warren's politics were Republican; but the political lines in California were far too fluid to make party identifications of great importance and Warren was about as non-partisan a party member as any governor could be. Each California candidate ran his campaign pretty largely by himself, and since Warren was by far the most popular political figure in the state, lesser known Republicans struggled to find ways of riding in on his coattails. As Governor, Warren appointed William Knowland to the Senate to fill a vacancy in 1945, but he put Knowland largely on his own when that Senator ran for the full term the next year. Warren's relations with Richard Nixon were never close, and he did not involve himself very deeply in Nixon's campaign for the Senate in 1950. Warren was himself twice re-elected as Governor, having the astonishing compliment of being nominated for his third term by both the Republican and the Democratic parties.

What were the ingredients of the Warren appeal? Here is a man who from 1925 to 1953 never lost an election in California. Living as he did in a state that was constantly changing, with ever-increasing problems, he could never simply coast on voting habits. Probably three-quarters of the people who voted for him in his last campaign were not even inhabitants of the state at the time of his first. The key ingredients of repeated victories were three:

1. He did his job honestly and effectively. There is no Warren scandal, no skeleton in the closet, nothing to be explained away.

2. He had a manner of dignified kinship with those he represented. He radiates sincerity of purpose, good will, and trust in others, the kind of trust which evokes trust in return. "The more we in public office trust the people, the more the people will trust us," he said, and he meant it; it was never Warren's way to ram things through but always to let them be discussed to a point of decision. At the same time, his was a dignified camaraderie. Without being stuffy, Warren was never the backslapping, sideshow performer type of politician.

3. Warren spoke for a deep-seated liberal tradition in California. California was progressive territory in Theodore Roosevelt's day. Its longtime Senator, Hiram Johnson, was one of the great progressives.

2 4

The Democratic Governors whom Warren followed were among the most liberal in the country. By taking a stand as a liberal Republican, Warren picked up the progressive strain of his own party, gave the Democrats nothing to complain about, and left more conservative Republicans with nowhere else to go. Warren was, at all times and at all places, an outspoken progressive. As he saw it, "a nation that abandons its social objectives is on the road to decadence. Within the limits of our financial means, every social objective of the American people must be advanced not only to relieve undue hardship and to afford equal opportunity for the good life, but also to demonstrate to an observing and critical world that our governmental and economic systems can work hand in hand in the elimination of poverty, suffering and degradation."

On the Supreme Court, Warren has been a consistent and vigorous supporter of the Bill of Rights, and of racial equality. The foundations of these views were all expressed when he was Governor of California. In 1947, he told the California Constitutional Convention that "the heart of any Constitution consists of its Bill of Rights, those provisions that secure to the people their liberty of conscience, of speech, of the press, of lawful assembly, and the right to uniform application of the laws and to due process of law. Every other provision of the Constitution should be designed in the spirit of these basic rights in order to make sure that they become not mere theoretical rights, but actual rights."

He spoke on equal rights in 1948 to a Jewish organization, saying, "Because intolerance has been directed against the Jews does not make it merely the problem of the Jews. Whenever and wherever intolerance rears its ugly head, it is the job of Americans—not of some Americans, but of all Americans—to suppress it."

The Governor was perfectly willing to take the unpopular side on this principle. When a Chinese in California moved into a neighborhood which seemed to be hostile to him, the Chinese decided to put it up to his potential new neighbors as to whether he should feel free to live there. The neighbors voted no. Warren wrote to the Chinese, "I am not at all proud of this action of the people in the neighborhood of your home. I am sure this is a disappointment to you and I agree with you that it is just such things that the Communists make much of in their effort to discredit our system."

In 1948, Warren made his first appearance in national politics as a candidate for Vice President with Thomas E. Dewey. The defeat following by President Truman was the only defeat Warren ever sustained as a candidate. In 1952, he actively sought the Republican presidential nomination. In that year, the fight was primarily between General Eisenhower and Senator Taft; but there was a possibility of a deadlock between the two and so a chance that Warren might be chosen. He had the California delegates solidly, or almost solidly, in his pocket. This was a block of seventy votes, enough to make a great difference to either of the main candidates. Under California law, the delegation was obligated to stand firm for Warren until he released it, and Senator Knowland, who led the delegation in Warren's behalf, issued strict instructions that no one in the delegation was to talk compromise with anyone.

But the then Senator Nixon had his own supporters within the California group. Amidst charges of "sellout," Nixon did give some indications to Governor Dewey and others behind the Eisenhower boom that he would be available himself for the Vice Presidency if Eisenhower was nominated. While the California delegation stood firm for Warren on the first ballot, the widespread impression that Nixon would lead a substantial secession toward Eisenhower undoubtedly assisted the General in picking up votes from other delegations which put him over on that ballot.

Though he was not nominated, Warren was still an immense power at home. In the campaign following, he was courted by both sides; the Democratic candidate, Governor Stevenson, saying good-naturedly at a Los Angeles appearance that "I think some Republicans are just about as good as Democrats. And, within that very limited category, I include the great Governor of this, my native state, Earl Warren." Warren, however, loyally backed his party's choice.

In January of 1953, General Eisenhower became President Eisenhower, and in September of the same year, Chief Justice Fred Vinson died. The President chose Warren for the succession. Eisenhower considered a number of other possibilities. Arthur T. Vanderbilt, Chief Justice of New Jersey, was certainly one, and according to one report, the President at least joked with his Secretary of State, John Foster Dulles, about the possibility of moving him over to the judicial job. One published account by a writer credited with inside information attributes the selection to Warren's prestige, to the fact that Eisenhower liked him personally and respected his integrity, and to the fact that Eisenhower liked his position on every issue which had come to his attention.

Warren came to the Supreme Court at the nadir of its fortunes. Chief Justice Stone, who had served in that capacity from 1941 to 1946, was a very great Justice, but far less successful in the special duties of a chief. Chief Justice Vinson, who followed him, was a man of splendid character and great dedication to his country, but had no particular talent for the business of being Chief Justice of the United States. The Court's opinion output had been on a downward spiral so that, for example, in the year 1950, the Court had decided fewer cases than in any year since 1850. Not since the term of Charles Evans Hughes, a truly great chief who stepped down in 1941, had there been a completely effective chief; and it was time for a strong hand at the helm.

Warren had not been on the Court a year when it fell to him to hand down the most momentous opinion of American life after World War II. On May 17, 1954, he spoke for the Court in a unanimous decision holding segregated education unconstitutional.

The Warren opinion was the final step in a course of legal development which had been under way for many years. The Civil War was followed by three constitutional Amendments. The Thirteenth gave the Negroes their freedom, the Fourteenth gave them the "equal protection of the laws," and the Fifteenth gave them the right to vote.

The key open question was just what they had received by the grant of "equal protection of the laws." Segregation, a device of enforced legal separation of whites and Negroes, largely began after the Civil War. Many who had sponsored the Fourteenth Amendment felt that this was a denial of equal protection, and in an early and little noticed post–Civil War decision, the Supreme Court did hold that separation even on an identical basis was not "equality."

But, by the end of the nineteenth century, the country and the Court had abandoned the fight. Segregation was upheld by the Supreme Court during the 1890's with only one Justice dissenting. Immediately thereafter, and on a rising spiral until the beginning of World War I, there was a great intensification of segregation in the United States. Whole new methods of separation were found, separation in stores, restaurants—everything, including cemeteries.

Beginning about 1920, the Supreme Court began to chip away at the separation concept. During the Chief Justiceship of Charles Evans Hughes in the 1930's, there was strict insistence that segregation, if it were to exist, must in truth be equal in fact. Before Chief Justice Warren came to the Court, two landmark decisions had been handed down, one that no state could require segregation in the holding of land and another holding that there could be no segregation in higher education.

The case before the Warren Court was the validity of segregation in primary schools. Every person participating in the case from beginning to end was aware of its momentous quality. The case was argued, and then reargued a year later. The briefs were prodigious. Every scrap of law or history or any other knowledge which could be offered to the Court was included. Any opinion which attempted seriously to canvass all these materials would have been hundreds of pages long.

Warren concluded to deal with the problem briefly. He began by recognizing that the best lesson history could teach was inconclusive.

Public school education in the Civil War period had not reached a point at which anyone gave much consideration to its relation to the meaning of the Fourteenth Amendment. By the 1950's conditions were very different. In our own time, said Warren, "education is perhaps the most important function of state and local governments. Compulsory school attendance laws and the great expenditures for education both demonstrate our recognition of the importance of education to our democratic society. It is required in the performance of our basic public responsibilities, even service in the armed forces. It is the very foundation of good citizenship." Undoubtedly, he said, the opportunity for education "is a right which must be made available to all on equal terms."

This brought him to the great question: "Does segregation of children in public schools solely on the basis of race, even though the physical facilities and other 'tangible' factors may be equal, deprive the children of the minority group of equal educational opportunities? We believe that it does." Referring to colored children, he said, "To separate them from others of similar age and qualifications solely because of their race generates a feeling of inferiority as to their status in the community that may affect their hearts and minds in a way unlikely ever to be undone." Segregation, continued Warren, necessarily instills a feeling of inferiority which would be bound to retard the educational and mental development of the children. Hence, "We conclude that in the field of public education the doctrine of 'separate but equal' has no place. Separate educational facilities are inherently unequal."

There remained the question of what was to be done about it. Warren and his fellow Justices were prepared to declare that segregated education was unconstitutional, but they also were anxious to give the segregated areas an adequate opportunity to adjust to the new order. How the decision was to be enforced was set for new argument, the practical effect being to postpone the decision itself for a year. At the end of this additional year, Warren in a second opinion declared that it was the duty of the trial courts to cause "a prompt and reasonable start toward full compliance." The trial courts were instructed to consider the problems of administration of school transportation, the revision of school districts, and all the other genuine difficulties of enforcement. But having taken all this into account, the trial courts were instructed to see to it that there should be school admissions on a racially non-discriminatory basis "with all deliberate speed."

The biggest work of the Warren Court has been these decisions and their aftermath. The immediate holding covered only the parties to the particular cases there involved, but new cases followed at once. President Eisenhower forthwith ordered desegregation of schools in the District of Columbia, and his order was carried out. Other areas voluntarily accepted the principle of the decision with more or less grace, notably Missouri, Kentucky, and West Virginia. But elsewhere there was turmoil, as new patterns began to emerge.

This is Warren's story, not an account of desegregation, and the details of that great excitement may be put aside. Nonetheless, the desegregation controversy has been for the balance of Warren's judicial career an everlastingly important offstage noise. All estimates of Warren, now and hereafter, are likely to be colored by attitudes on this. Case after case has come up on the same theme, segregation in restaurants, on golf courses, on buses, and in schools, and more schools. The tremendous triumph of Warren and the Warren Court together is that it has been able to stand as a unit for ten years on all these topics with almost no divisions within itself. The process of desegregation has been difficult and frequently tragic and ugly. It might have been an impossibility if the Court had not consistently spoken with but one voice. The simple and precise adherence of the Court to its position in case after case is a credit to each individual Justice, but it is also attributable to Warren as a distinct leadership accomplishment. By 1962 the Court had buried the segregation question as deep as it is ever possible to bury a constitutional issue, holding that the unconstitutionality of segregation was so overwhelmingly established that it was no longer open to discussion.

Meanwhile, the Court had much other business to concern it. There was the administration of the whole federal legal system of which Warren rapidly took hold. There was the matter of bringing the Court back to a reasonable productivity, which also occurred. But another great issue of the day arose from the activities of legislative committees which, in the course of investigating possible subversive activities menacing the United States, appeared frequently to focus on exposure for its own sake. This in turn led to character destruction, which in some cases might be completely unjustified. An offhand observation which Warren made early in his service, while not having the polish of an opinion, expressed his point of view: "To the extent that anyone indiscriminately charges individuals or groups of individuals with dishonesty or subversion or whatever it might be that would destroy a reputation, that is, in my opinion, not in the American tradition and should not be encouraged."

Warren certainly did not encourage it. In a 1957 opinion, he made very clear that the Congressional power of investigation is extremely broad, "But broad as is this power of inquiry, it is not unlimited. There is no general authority to expose the private affairs of individuals without justification in terms of the functions of the Congress." As he saw it, the Congress is not "a law enforcement or trial agency . . . investigations conducted solely for the personal aggrandizement of the investigators or to 'punish' those investigated are indefensible."

The two cases just discussed—the segregation case and the legislative investigation case—illustrate a range of Warren techniques. The segregation case is brief. It dealt with a matter on which the country had been in debate for many years. No further talk could be fruitful. It was a time to state conclusions concisely, and the Court did. The investigation matter on the other hand was one on which the country was not fully informed. There was a need for education both for Congress and for the public. Warren dealt with the subject comprehensively, fully considering the function of legislative investigations from earliest to most recent times. The opinion is not only a decision, it is an education.

The key to the Warren attitude in the investigation case is his observation that trials are for the Courts. The phrase reveals one of the deepest premises of Warren's whole character. He is a man who believes in due process of law with a spirit of complete attachment. To understand the Warren of today, one must never forget that he was a county attorney for twenty years of his life. Not the most experienced of his brethren on the Court—and several have very substantial experience in criminal matters—can come close to equaling the intensity of his experience. He knows precisely what a good, fair, orderly trial is and he is determined that every American accused of crime shall have one.

Warren wants trials to be trials, and not sideshows. This is why he feels so intensely that television and photography should stay out of the courtrooms. It is scarcely too extreme to say that the first photographer or broadcaster who gets into a federal court will have to do so over the dead body of the Chief Justice. In 1962, when the then head of the Federal Communications Commission recommended that radio and television should be allowed into courtrooms and proposed that the American Bar Association should relax its standards in this regard, the Chief Justice gave the matter deep thought. The result was the adoption by the Judicial Conference of a clear-cut directive that under no circumstances would there be pictures or broadcasts in the federal courts; and this strong position so firmly buttressed the American Bar Association's position that it is unlikely that there will be any change in the states. So far as Warren is concerned, the person accused of crime has enough on his mind without worrying about how he is going to look to the curious.

In matters of trial procedure, Warren draws on his experience as a district attorney for highly practical distinctions. Take the two cases of secret electrical recording. In the first, decided before Warren came to the Court, a government agent with a small portable broadcaster up his sleeve engaged a defendant in a conversation. The conversation, unknown to the defendant, was being transmitted and recorded at a nearby point. The recording was used against the defendant without having the agent available for cross-examination. In the second case, an agent also engaged the defendant in a conversation secretly recorded by a pocket device. In this case the agent did appear and was subject to cross-examination, and the recording served only as confirmation or added proof of the agent's testimony.

When this second case came before the Court in 1963, Warren thought the second practice constitutionally acceptable and the first not. He recognized "that the fantastic advances in the field of electronic communication constitute a great danger to the privacy of the individual." In the first case, the agent was not present; if he had been examined, the whole matter might have looked different. In the second case, the recording simply served to defend the agent from a charge that he was not telling the truth. Warren thought this only fair, saying: "In the performance of their duty, agents are thus often faced with situations where proof of an attempted bribe will be a matter of their word against that of a tax evader and perhaps some of his associates. They should not be defenseless against outright denials or claims of entrapment, claims which if not open to conclusive refutations will undermine the reputation of the individual agent for honesty and the public's confidence in his work. When confronted with such a situation, it is only fair that an agent be permitted to support his credibility with a recording as agent Davis did in this case."

One of Warren's key jobs is to serve as Chairman of the Conference of the Justices. Here he makes a preliminary statement of each case. To prepare himself, he has his clerks make memos on each of the applications to be heard. He then reviews their notes and the actual papers. He makes a few handwritten notes on each case, a sort of shorthand of his own which no one else could read, in which one letter may stand for a word and a couple of letters for a phrase. Possessed of these notes, he outlines the problem to the Court. If there are practical as well as legal consequences to the ruling, he brings those out as well. He then gives his recommendation to the Court and passes the discussion on to the next Justice.

In preparing his decisions Warren's system is to dictate a memorandum in every case which someone else might call a first draft but which he regards simply as a memorandum. Then he calls in one of his clerks and goes over the memorandum with him for as much as two or three hours and studies the briefs. All oral arguments are recorded as they are made and Warren may play them back at this point. He then has his clerk prepare a second draft based on the extensive discussion and on the memo from which they started. This second draft is then worked and reworked as may be necessary. When the opinion itself is finally ready to be released, Warren regularly replays the oral argument in full. He recognizes that he can't always remember every detail, and something may turn up on that last replay which shows that he had missed something important.

Warren conceives of the Supreme Court in relation to the courts of the country as he conceives of his own handling of his own work. The job is leadership plus delegation. He recognizes that most of the decisions must be made by the federal courts of appeal and takes great satisfaction in what he thinks is their thorough co-operation. He feels that these lower federal judges are doing their best to keep acquainted with the Supreme Court's rulings and to carry them out. At the same time, Warren feels that Supreme Court Justices have no spare time and he thinks it extremely undesirable for them to engage in any avoidable non-judicial work. Hence, it was with the most extreme reluctance that he accepted the request of President Johnson to head the Commission investigating the assassination of President Kennedy. However, he was persuaded by President Johnson that his acceptance of the assignment was absolutely essential to the public interest.

Because Warren has been a vigorous leader of a vigorous Court, he has been subject to an extraordinary degree of personal vilification.

He is a favorite target of the extremists of the far right. The John Birch Society would love to impeach him, and he is a favorite object of attack of extreme segregationists.

None of this troubles the Chief particularly. He enjoys his work on the Court and his association with his colleagues. He has a splendid personal relationship with all those currently serving. He married Nina Meyers in 1925, and she is his constant companion; and he takes keen interest in his six children and his grandchildren.

Certainly the Birchers are not moving Warren from the path of his convictions. In a 1963 decision, he held that the House Committee on Un-American Activities had failed to comply with its own rules and that therefore a witness before it was excused from answering its questions. He has governed himself from the beginning to the end of his public service by principles he expressed in a lecture at New York University in 1962:

I am one who believes firmly that the Court must be vigilant against neglect of the requirements of our Bill of Rights and the personal rights that document was intended to guarantee for all time. . . . Democracy under our Constitution calls for judicial deference to the co-ordinate branches of the Government and their judgment of what is essential to the protection of the Nation. But it follows no less for a steadfast protection of those fundamentals imbedded in the Constitution, so incorporated for the express purpose of insulating them from possible excesses of the moment.

But while Warren finds Birch Society picket lines no more than unpleasant, he does as a calm and reasonable man regret the rise of passions and intemperateness as a national vice. He spoke of this at the ceremony over the body of the late President Kennedy:

We are saddened; we are stunned; we are perplexed.
John Fitzgerald Kennedy, a great and good President, the friend of all men of good will, a believer in the dignity and equality of all human beings, a fighter for justice, and apostle of peace, has been snatched from our midst by the bullet of an assassin.
What moved some misguided wretch to do this horrible deed may

35

never be known to us, but we do know that such acts are commonly stimulated by forces of hatred and malevolence, such as today are eating their way into the bloodstream of American life.

What a price we pay for this fanaticism.

It has been said that the only thing we learn from history is that we do not learn. But surely we can learn if we have the will to do so. Surely there is a lesson to be learned from this tragic event.

If we really love this country, if we truly love justice and mercy, if we fervently want to make this Nation better for those who are to follow us, we can at least abjure the hatred that consumes people, the false accusations that divide us, and the bitterness that begets violence.

Is it too much to hope that the martyrdom of our beloved President might even soften the hearts of those who would themselves recoil from assassination, but who do not shrink from spreading the venom which kindles thoughts of it in others?

The Chief Justice has had less opportunity than a President to be an apostle for peace; but surely he too has been the friend of all men of good will, a believer in the dignity and equality of all human beings, and a fighter for justice.

Chapter Three

MR. JUSTICE
Hugo L. Black

IN 1942, the Supreme Court decided the case of *Betts* v. *Brady.* Justice Black's dissent gives the facts: "The petitioner, a farmhand, out of a job and on relief was indicted in a Maryland state court on a charge of robbery. He was too poor to hire a lawyer. He so informed the court and requested that counsel be appointed to defend him. His request was denied. Put to trial without a lawyer, he conducted his own defense, was found guilty and was sentenced to eight years' imprisonment. The Court below found that the petitioner had 'at least an ordinary amount of intelligence.' It is clear from his examination of witnesses that he was a man of little education."

The issue was whether, when a man is too poor to obtain a lawyer for his own defense, the state is obligated to appoint someone for him. Black said that no practice is fair "which subjects innocent men to increased dangers of conviction merely because of their poverty. Whether a man is innocent cannot be determined from a trial in which, as here, denial of counsel has made it impossible to conclude, with any satisfactory degree of certainty, that the defendant's case was adequately presented." He believed that no man should be deprived of counsel because he was poor—"any other practice seems to me to defeat the promise of democratic society to provide equal justice under the law."

In *Betts* v. *Brady,* a majority of the Court disagreed and held that a man could be convicted in a state court, even though he had no lawyer to defend him simply because he was poor. There is probably no single opinion of the Supreme Court between 1940 and 1964 which has seemed more wrong to more Americans who knew of its existence than this one. It does not take a generation nurtured on Perry Mason to realize that a man charged with a serious offense needs help. Almost any American who asks himself whether he would want and need a lawyer if he were charged with an offense will agree with Justice Black. The law is a complicated business and a man may be the soul of innocence and still want the aid of a lawyer in his hour of need. For most Americans, the most astonishing feature of *Betts* v. *Brady* is that the Court could have so decided in the first place.

For twenty-one years, Black kept chipping away. He reiterated his dissent time after time. Bit by bit the rule of *Betts* v. *Brady* was narrowed and confined. In more and more cases, the right to counsel was upheld.

Finally, in 1963, came the day. A man named Gideon was charged with having broken into a poolroom. He had no funds to retain a lawyer, and he asked that one be appointed. The case arose in Florida which did not then appoint counsel for the poor. Gideon's case found its way to the Supreme Court on exactly the same issue as *Betts* v. *Brady*. This time it was Justice Black who spoke, not for the dissenters, but for the Court.

Black recognized that Gideon's case was substantially the same as *Betts,* and concluded that, "upon full reconsideration we conclude that *Betts* v. *Brady* should be overruled." The right to counsel was a fundamental right, said Black, for "reason and reflection require us to recognize that in our adversary system of criminal justice, any person haled into court, who is too poor to hire a lawyer, cannot be assured a fair trial unless counsel is provided for him. This seems to us to be an obvious truth." Governments spend immense amounts of money to prosecute criminals, and the defendants who can afford it invariably get the best lawyers they can find. He continued:

The right of one charged with crime to counsel may not be fundamental and essential to fair trials in some countries, but it is in ours. From the very beginning, our state and national constitutions and laws have laid great emphasis on procedural and substantive safeguards designed to assure fair trials before impartial tribunals in which every defendant stands equal before the law. This noble idea cannot be realized if the poor man charged with crime has to face his accusers without a lawyer to assist him.

If ever a man was entitled to savor a triumph, it was Hugo Black on that day. It had been a twenty-one-year war, and he had won it. Yet he did not pause for even one moment of purely personal satisfaction. For this, there are two reasons. First, Black is, in his basic character, not the kind of a man who takes personal pride in besting an adversary, whether that adversary be an idea or an individual.

Second, Black's has been a career which makes him used to triumphs. He is now virtually the senior statesman of the United States. Very few figures in American public life can match his thirty-seven years, ten in the Senate and twenty-seven on the Supreme Court. When Black came to the Senate, more than half of his colleagues of the present Supreme Court were not yet graduated from law school. Some of them had not yet begun college. In so long a span, one may become used to victory.

No single individual has more sharply put his own personal imprint upon the law as declared by the Supreme Court from 1937 to the present day than Justice Black. Probably not a half-dozen Justices in the entire history of the Court have had comparable personal impact. This volume began with a list of areas in which the Court had been particularly dynamic during the years of the Warren Chief Justiceship. Let us review them in relation to Justice Black:

1. Segregation. Here the leadership has been that of the Chief Justice with Black, the Justice from the deepest South, supporting him all the way.

2. Equal representation for all Americans in state legislatures and Congress. After segregation, this is the most important area of the Court's work during the Warren years. This is *Betts* v. *Brady* all over again—in this field of fair representation, today's Court has adopted

what was Black's earlier position in dissent and made it the law. His basic 1964 opinion requiring substantially equal Congressional districts is accelerating the reconstruction of the House of Representatives.

3. Separation of church and state. Here the basic opinions are by Black.

4. To ensure fair trial by eliminating forced confessions by insisting upon the right to counsel. The leading opinions on forced confessions are by Black and the leading opinions on right to counsel are by Black.

5. Enforcement of the antitrust laws. Black has been strongly with others, though by no means alone, in leading this development.

6. Free speech and the recovery from McCarthyism. Black, along with Justice Douglas, fought the restrictions in individual liberty in the 1946–1954 period every step of the way. Across this broad front, his views are beginning to prevail.

7. Improved procedure and administration and supervision of the federal courts. This, Black has not dealt with.

8. Disposal of an immense number of other cases. For more than twenty-five years, Black has been one of the workhorses of the Court, turning out his full share of opinions and more for all these years.

This, then, is the titan of the modern law: the son of a country storekeeper from a village in rural Alabama, a man who today at the age of seventy-eight plays a good set of tennis for exercise and takes his principal pleasure in the company of his wife and his three children and their families. These are his son, Hugo, who practices law in Miami, Florida; his son, Sterling, who practices law in Los Alamos, New Mexico; and his daughter, Josephine, who is married to a psychiatrist in Bergen County, New Jersey. Black can still regularly put in ten hours a day on Court work.

For above all else, Black is energy.

That energy is, as ever, rigidly controlled. One of the early surprises to Black's close associates is his capacity to listen. An energetic man whose trade is in the verbal arts tends to be talkative. If fame has touched him, making him automatically the lion of a group, he is ofttimes voluble; and if all this is combined with age, the result is commonly a flow, downright irrepressible. Black, whose fluency and energy are in good part the basis of his career, can listen to a lawyer, a clerk, a stranger, or a friend, with absorption. He will say his say when his turn comes.

This energy control, even in the minor affairs of life, is an example of Black's adjustment to the world. He has the capacity to commit himself with zest to whatever he is doing at the moment. He is intensely interested in his work, but it never becomes a monomania. He plays tennis as though his life depended on it, but does not talk the game away from the court. As an insatiable gardener, with equal devotion to his roses, his fig trees, his corn and his grapes, he immerses himself in the most patient of hobbies. In this, perhaps, he is only re-creating his boyhood home, where Burpee's seed catalog was the book used second only to the Bible.

While Black's background was limiting and, in the most exact sense, provincial, Clay County, Alabama, his boyhood home, was no Tobacco Road, and Black is no splinter of white trash who made good. His circumstances, while such as to make him self-dependent at an early age, were not more severe than those of some of his colleagues on the Bench. Indeed, his affectionate and easy relationship with Chief Justice Warren may rest in part on the circumstance that each has come up the ladder from approximately the same rung, and has been unspoiled by the ascent. One trace of this climb is his continuing desire to help others along the road: his choice of law clerks is frequently dictated more by considerations of whom he can help than of who can help him. As Charles Beard puts it, "In all the annals of the Court, it would be difficult, if not impossible, to find another Justice so intimately acquainted with the disadvantages [the poor] encountered in the struggle for existence."

As a boy, from his birth on February 27, 1886, he led the normal life of an Alabama villager, and did the usual odd jobs. His later skill with words may have been foreshadowed by the fact that he was a better odd-hour typesetter at the local printshop than he was a cotton-picker. In this atmosphere, he learned politics, absorbing his first impressions when the Populists and William Jennings Bryan were seeking the vote.

After a touch of high-school-type education at an institution glorified by the name of Ashland College, and following a dab of medical training, Black went to the University of Alabama Law School at the age of eighteen. It was not his first choice—he would have preferred to enter a liberal-arts course, but the University found his credits inadequate. He went to law school, in short, because he was too poorly educated to go anywhere else. As one of his professors put it, Black "had the most to learn" of anyone in the school. He learned a good share of it, making the small school's honors list.

After a brief try in Ashland, where a fire in his office put an end to his efforts to get rich on fifty-cent fees, he moved to Birmingham, broadened his acquaintance by joining every organization that would take him, and began a general practice. In a few years, he was judge of a criminal court of petty jurisdiction, a post that began to give him his extraordinary insight into criminal-law enforcement. A term as prosecuting attorney before World War I did much to complete the job.

The result is that when Black writes on criminal procedure, he has seen what he is talking about. *Habeas corpus* or bail? When Black took over the prosecutor's desk, the Birmingham jail was full of people being held indefinitely awaiting trial, and earning extra food fees for a rapacious sheriff in the meantime. Black cleaned out the crowd and learned from observation the meaning of a speedy trial. Third degree? Black obtained his first touch of national notice—and some local criticism—when he broke up the third-degree practices of the law-enforcement authorities in Bessemer, Alabama, where it was not uncommon to tie a Negro to a door and lash him with a belt buckle until he confessed. Black prepared a grand jury report on the Bessemer outrages which concluded:

Such practices are dishonorable, tyrannical, and despotic, and such rights must not be surrendered to any officer or set of officers, so long as human life is held sacred and human liberty and human safety of paramount importance.

In Birmingham, Black learned the practical ways of sympathy for the unfortunate. A Negro who created a disturbance because of marital troubles might get off with a lecture on happy marriage from the young bachelor judge, but an old fraud who sold high-priced "charms" to the Negroes got full penalty. In his later role Black prosecuted a coal company that deprived its employees of fair pay by short-weighting them; and he put pressure on insurance companies to keep them from obtaining premature releases from injured employees. Still later, as a Supreme Court Justice, Black was to strive to make such releases less attractive to those who obtained them, but it is doubtful whether he has to this day brought his brother Justices to share his feelings to the full.

An Army interlude in World War I started a ten-year interruption in Black's officeholding career. When he came back, a captain experienced in battle only on the parade grounds of an Oklahoma training camp, he settled down to the business of building a practice, making money, and taking a wife.

At all three he was a success. The greatest success was his marriage to Josephine Foster, a Birmingham girl of good family, great vivacity, and extraordinary charm. The home she made for her husband and their three children was a sanctuary from the political battles of the years to come, and in later days her table sparkled with some of the gayest, as well as some of the best, conversation in Washington. Her death was Black's darkest hour.

Black's postwar practice boomed. As a jury lawyer, Black was one of the small circle of the unequaled great. Between 1919 and 1928, Black's firm had over one hundred cases in the Alabama Supreme Court, mostly for injuries, and Black's biggest task was to hold the judgments he had induced juries to give. Fifty thousand dollars for an injured railroad worker was cut to thirty thousand by the court, and twenty-five thousand for an eye injury dropped to six thousand on review. As the Alabama court observed in one instance, Black had fully demonstrated "his ability to eloquently present the cause in the most forcible manner."

Black as a jury lawyer was no poseur given to chuckling in his office at, for example, the jury who the Alabama Supreme Court said had "been rather too liberal with the money of the defendant." The sincerity that was part of his stock in trade was genuine: in his eyes tort juries were instruments of justice too often frustrated by judges. He brought to the Supreme Court a determination to free juries of these limitations, and almost certainly he has done more than any other man to restore to juries in the twentieth century some of the freedom they had in the nineteenth.

The jury controversy bubbles quietly in the Supreme Court, unmarked by the flashing sensationalism of such problems as race relations or free speech, in which individual cases can be monumental. But Black's interest has caused the Court to take up a far greater portion of the Federal Employers' Liability Act and other federal jury cases than before; and today in both federal courts and state courts following the federal lead, there is much more jury latitude than in 1940. He himself, although he has not quite denied that the judge can *ever* take a case from a jury or set aside a jury verdict, at least has not seen a case during his service on the Court where this was properly done. To him, the Seventh Amendment is as much to be honored as any other constitutional provision:

The call for the true application of the Seventh Amendment is not to words, but to the spirit of honest desire to see that constitutional right preserved. Either the judge or the jury must decide facts and, to the extent that we take this responsibility, we lessen the jury function. . . . As for myself, I believe that a verdict should be directed, if at all, only when, without weighing the credibility of the witnesses, there is in the evidence no room whatever for honest difference of opinion over the factual issue in controversy. I shall continue to believe that in all other cases a judge should, in obedience to the command of the Seventh Amendment, not interfere with the jury's function.

By 1926, Black could afford financially to run for the Senate. After a grueling race against three candidates, each of whom had far more money and organized support than he, Black was elected. The keys to victory were two: Black's own background and views gave him a genuine appeal to the common people of the state that no other candidate could equal; and his endless vigor took him out among the voters at a pace no other candidate could follow.

As a campaigner, Black was rough and direct, making a straight class appeal to the common man as one of their own. He stressed his Clay County origins, his absence of railroad, power company, and corporate connections. He was, in fact, as he said, the "candidate of the masses." As one weekly paper put the spirit that elected him, "he knows better how to sympathize with the common people."

Black campaigned for full public use of Muscle Shoals and for prohibition enforcement. He never, despite a short previous dalliance with the Klan, later sensationalized, followed the Klan's line. It supported two of his opponents in the 1926 race, and after his later alliance with Catholic Tom Walsh in the Senate, his support of Al Smith in 1928, and his opposition to the Klan's idol Tom Heflin in 1930, the Klan was his flat enemy in the re-election campaign of 1932.

Black's support of public power and fertilizer production at the Shoals was popular in Alabama, particularly in the northern portions of the state, and his prohibition stand was that of most Alabamans. Both personally and politically, his prohibitionism was ardent. Black's own family had seen vivid evidence of the evils of drink during his boyhood. While time has brought him to believe that drinking cannot be stopped by statute—and, indeed, he now takes one drink a day himself at a doctor's suggestion, though with no perceptible pleasure— he doubtless still regrets that this is so. Of the noble purpose of the great experiment, he has never had any doubts.

Once in the Senate, Black set out to educate himself. He was, it must be remembered, still an essentially uneducated man, with little better than a bad high school training. The Senate became his university; George Norris and Bronson Cutting, two of his professors; and the Library of Congress, his bookshelf. Today the *Annals* of Tacitus are at his fingertips, his many-volumed Livy is thoroughly marked with his jottings, and evidences of Macaulay crop up again and again in his opinions. Such self-education took great effort, and left no time for idle occupancy of the Senate floor. As the Mobile *Register* put it, "Alabama makes a good senatorial average, with one senator [Heflin] talking incessantly, and one not at all."

In ten senatorial years, spanning the transition from complete Republican dominion under Coolidge and Hoover to the peak of New Deal ascendancy, Black became an established leader of the most militant liberal group. The Senate of the United States is a co-operative body, and it is rare that one Senator can fairly claim total credit for any one accomplishment. Black would certainly not do so. But he played important roles in three major New Deal measures:

1. The establishment of the TVA, in which Black was an effective lieutenant of George Norris.

2. The adoption of the Public Utility Holding Company Act of 1935—the Wheeler-Rayburn Act—which almost certainly would never have succeeded without the Black lobby investigation. That investigation made him a nationwide sensation as he revealed the almost incredible devices of the utilities opposing the bill, including forged telegrams and petitions, bribes, and million-dollar advertising campaigns which extended to direct corruption of newspapers. The backlash of this investigation made Black one of the most hated of the New Dealers as well as one of the most effective. He became the *bête noire* of the Hearst press, particularly as his investigations went on into the Liberty League in 1936. Raymond Clapper wrote in 1935, "If the death sentence finally goes into the utilities bill, it will be another notch in the gun of Hugo Black."

3. The enactment of the Wage-Hour Act of 1938 which, while it passed after Black's Supreme Court appointment and is the product also of many other hands, was a direct result of his years of agitation for a thirty-hour-week bill. Black, greatly influenced by the English economist G. D. H. Cole, and himself a thorough student of European social legislation, had long campaigned against low Southern wages. To him, the once dominant Southern viewpoint that wages of eight

cents to twenty cents an hour were among the blessings of God to the South was "indefensible. I do not believe our civilization requires any such sacrifice on the part of any large percentage of our people."

Today there are few who would doubt that the TVA and the Wage-Hour law are fundamental to the prosperity of the South; and the passing of the Insulls and the Hopsons of the holding-company era is mourned by none. Black was a significant member of the team that wrought these accomplishments. In the Wage-Hour fight he was forced to proclaim that he was as good a Southerner as the best of them, with as great a loyalty to Dixie and with as many ancestors in the Civil War. The event proves that he saw his region's interest truly. Another twenty years may show that in his persistent opposition to segregation he was equally foreseeing the eventual welfare of the southeastern states, which he unashamedly loves and in which he spends as much as possible of his life.

On the evening of August 11, 1937, Senator Black went to the White House at the request of the President. It had already been quietly intimated to him by Sherman Minton, his friend and colleague in the Senate and later on the Court, that the President would offer Black the Supreme Court vacancy created by the resignation of Willis Van Devanter. The next day, President Roosevelt sent the name of Hugo Lafayette Black to the Senate.

No one could say that it was, in the superficial sense, a popular appointment. The Court-packing fight had just been fought and lost, with Black supporting the President every inch of the way. Today the Supreme Court no longer has the force of the conservative-controlled organs of public opinion solidly behind it, but in 1937, the Court was the last stronghold of the political and economic forces that had been repeatedly defeated at the polls. From the viewpoint of the vehicles of opinion that these forces controlled—vehicles that already had every reason to hate Black—the President's attack on the Court had been as sacrilegious as an attack on a Vestal Virgin might have seemed to a Roman. Now that one attack had been fought off, to get Black on the Court would be to lose everything that had been saved—a thought that almost certainly occurred to the President, with reverse twist, when he made his selection.

And so no one ever took the Bench with a worse press. But there were occasional contrary notes. The labor unions the country over were for Black. Even the Canadian delegation at a boilermakers' convention asked the privilege of recording their "faith and confidence" in the Justice. George Norris, long the grand old man of American liberalism, said:

He is a worthy representative of the common people. He understands their hopes and ambitions, and their liberties in his hands will be safe.

By now, we can measure the validity of the Norris forecast. Has Black been a worthy representative of the common people? The concept is mystical, and necessarily the measure must be subjective; different generations may give different answers. But there has been time enough since 1937 for some perspective to develop. We can now dimly perceive that the thirties were the climax of an American revolution with deep roots; that the enemy to be overthrown was economic anarchy; and that the insurgents were the farmers and industrial workers of the country, in particular, seeking to take over the management of the nation's economy. Hugo Black was one of the captains of that revolution; he was a strong force in it. And he, of those in the New Deal tide who reached the Bench of the Supreme Court of the United States, was the one who most clearly in personal origins and career was himself a true part of the farmer-labor movement.

On the Supreme Court, Justice Black has been a consistent year in and year out representative of the economic aspirations of the common man. This does not mean that in particular cases his judgment has necessarily coincided with immediate group interests; other values sometimes conflict. A notable example was his *Bethlehem Steel* decision, which left to Bethlehem some highly inflated gains of World War I, but in so doing precipitated the more rigorous profit controls of World War II. Similarly in the *Steel Seizure* case, his conclusion that the President might not seize private property in peacetime was, in the immediate situation, to labor's disadvantage; yet in a longer view it is approximately as much a protection to labor as it is to all other groups. But the overwhelming bulk of Black's decisions on economic matters, within such real limits of policy as there are in the business of judging, are about what the great mass of Americans (at least in the thirties) would have wanted if they could clearly have understood the stakes. Black has well understood their "hopes and ambitions" in the antitrust and other trade regulations, the labor, and the agricultural matters before the Court.

More important, in his hands, as Senator Norris said, their liberties have been safe. The greatest single problem raised by the creation of a welfare state has been that a state aggressive enough to regularize the economy may also be aggressive enough to regularize human thought, or advocacy, or behavior in areas that, in the earlier American tradition, were none of the business of the state. A clear example is the application of the commerce power to vitalize labor unions followed by the extension of regulation to control the views of their officers. Many a conservative of the 1930's predicted that personal liberty would fall with the expansion of government, and today many an early enthusiast for the age of reform fears that these critics may have been alarmingly right.

For all these years, Justice Black has preached the doctrine that the government should at the same time be both all-powerful and all-weak; that over the economy it should have all the power needed to cope with the problems of each day, and that over the thought, speech, and spirit of the citizen it should have no power at all.

This much at least of what he conceives to be the Jeffersonian tradition, the Justice has systematically carried into our times. No one ever scared harder; and his faith in the redoubtable qualities of the Republic enables him to be unconcerned at the sea of political perils that, we are so regularly told, surrounds us.

Justice Black is the extreme proponent in public life of the view that there should be no restrictions whatsoever on freedom of speech. Since the days in the Senate when he opposed the practice of censoring books imported from abroad, he has adhered to the simple view that the First Amendment is the greatest of American liberties, and that the words "no law abridging the freedom of speech, or of the press" mean, quite simply, that there should be no law that abridges either. The Amendment is, he has said,

precise enough to mark out an area over which Government should have no power at all. . . . The language of the First Amendment indicates to me that the Founders weighed the risks involved in such freedoms and deliberately chose to stake this Government's security and life upon preserving liberty to discuss public affairs intact and untouchable by government.

In the years from about 1946 to about 1954, the country spent an astonishing amount of its energies to ensure that the Communists would not capture it. That wholesome objective was pursued with rather more exuberance than the necessity warranted, and as a result, a good many innocent people and a good many traditional American liberties took a severe beating. This is the phenomenon generally remembered, if not esteemed, under the label "McCarthyism." Throughout those years Justices Black and Douglas were the foremost opponents in the United States of the repressionist drive. As the representatives of the American far right are fond of saying, these two Justices have not a 90 per cent, not a 95 per cent, but a 100 per cent record of opposition to their goals and the means which they have chosen to achieve them.

There have been times when any possible recovery of the Black-Douglas point of view has seemed almost hopeless. Perhaps Black's best statement was a 1959 dissent, joined by the Chief Justice and Justice Douglas, in the case of a contempt conviction of a man who had refused to answer questions concerning his political activities when he had been a student at the University of Michigan some ten years before. Black believed that the Committee could not compel the witness to answer these questions; that under the Constitution he had a right to be silent as an element of his right of freedom of speech. A few words will give the flavor of Black's opinion: "The First Amendment says in no equivocal language that Congress shall pass no law abridging freedom of speech, press, assembly or petition. The activities of this Committee authorized by Congress, do precisely that, through exposure, obloquy and public scorn."

Black referred to the words of James Madison that the Bill of Rights should protect against every encroachment upon the rights of American citizens. He denounced the position of the government that it had the power to control "communication of unlawful ideas." Black said that no ideas could be made wrongful under our Constitution. He stated his basic faith in these words:

Our Constitution assumes that the common sense of the people in their attachment to their country will enable them, after free discussion, to withstand ideas that are wrong. To say that our patriotism must be protected against false ideas by means other than these is, I think, to make a baseless charge. Unless we can rely on these qualities —if, in short, we begin to punish speech—we cannot honestly proclaim ourselves to be a free Nation and we have lost what the Founders of this land risked their lives and their sacred honor to defend.

He concluded sadly, "Today's holding, in my judgment, marks another major step in the progressively increasing retreat from the safeguards of the First Amendment."

Much of the subsiding of the McCarthy excesses are due to resurgent common sense of the American people themselves; but some are also due to the consistent teachings of Justices Black and Douglas and to the adoption of their point of view in many of the Court's decisions in recent years.

In the course of almost forty years of public life, crises and attacks have become such old stuff to Black that he takes them in easy stride. The most recent followed his opinion in the New York Regents prayer case. The Regents, controllers of education in the State of New York, had directed that all school children should begin each day with a prayer, "Almighty God, we acknowledge our dependence upon Thee, and we beg Thy blessings upon us, our parents, our teachers and our country." This prayer is surely innocuous enough, a kind of thin gruel of a prayer with very little nourishment for the religious and very little offense to the rest of the community. But if the state can prescribe one prayer it can prescribe another. Black, in an opinion for the Court holding the prayer improper in the schools, declared that the Constitution was a guarantee that "neither the power nor the prestige of the Federal Government would be used to control, support or influence the kinds of prayer the American people can say—that the people's religions must not be subjected to the pressures of government for change each time a new political administration is elected to office." And the same rule applied to the states.

As Black saw it, the business of prayer is for the home and the church: "It is neither sacrilegious nor antireligious to say that each separate government in this country should stay out of the business of writing or sanctioning official prayers and leave that purely religious function to the people themselves and to those the people choose to look to for religious guidance." He concluded that "it is no part of the business of government to compose official prayers for any group of the American people to recite as a part of a religious program carried on by government."

The attack was venomous. Constitutional amendments were immediately introduced in Congress to reverse the results. Black himself was maligned as he had not been for many years. And yet, as Professor Philip Kurland, of the University of Chicago Law School, observed soon after the decision: "It is hard to believe that many who now find this notion unpalatable will not soon, or eventually, be applauding it. A contrary result . . . could easily have authorized the reading in school ceremony of a version of the New Testament that is offensive to some students." He continued, "Indeed, when time gives the opportunity for thoughtful evaluation, rather than emotional reaction, [this case] may come to be recognized as one of the bulwarks of America's freedom from the ills that continue to plague those countries where 'toleration' rather than 'freedom' and 'separation' are the guides to government action."

So it has swiftly proved. Many religious leaders around the country soon came to conclude that empty prayers of the Regents variety, in fact, serve no godly purpose; and yet the capacity to prescribe this prayer might very easily be construed to be a capacity to prescribe a great deal more. Such leaders concluded that they would rather keep prayer out of the schools altogether. The proposed constitutional Amendments were allowed quietly to die. When, a year later, the Court followed Black's opinion with a second holding that the Lord's Prayer should not be read in public schools, the decision was generally accepted. Soon the wise perception spread over the country that any prayer which was so innocuous as to be inoffensive to all of the many American religions was in its very best nature bound to be empty; and any prayer with substance was sure to be obnoxious to some.

What of the Black of 1964, seventy-eight years of age, with twenty-seven years on the Supreme Court? In 1951, the Justice's first wife died. What followed were years of unremitting gloom. For a man for whom the Washington social routine had never been important and whose pleasure had always been taken in his family and a small circle of friends, the loneliness was nearly unendurable. His friends grieved sorrowfully for what seemed to be the dreary finish of a joyous life.

Then came the change. The Justice fell very much in love with his secretary, Elizabeth Seay DeMeritte, an Alabama woman and herself a still youthful grandmother. To the accompaniment of "I've Grown Accustomed to Your Face," the Justice and Mrs. DeMeritte began a new life with a marriage in 1957.

The Justice became again a genuinely happy man, with bounce restored to his step, and a whistle, and sometimes full bursts of song on his lips. The result has been a perfectly extraordinary rebirth. In 1956, when the Justice was seventy, I wrote a birthday piece which in thinly veiled tone anticipated early retirement. Today that thought is not even on the horizon. After President Kennedy's assassination in November, 1963, and Chief Justice Warren's involvement in the Commission of Investigation, the Court duties of Black as senior Associate Justice increased. His output was substantial, its quality high.

53

The record for Supreme Court service is thirty-five years, and Black at seventy-eight shows every sign of being able to break it.

In terms of work habits, his ways remain largely as they have been. Twenty years ago he always did the first draft of every opinion, turning the draft over to the clerk to make the second. The second draft, which was usually filled in by the clerk with supplemental authorities and details and sometimes revised a little as to order, was then returned to Black who, if the case was of substance, prepared a third draft. The clerk then took another turn at it, and the fourth draft was likely to be gone over by the two aloud, word for word and detail for detail, to achieve the twin objectives of perfect clarity and tight brevity. Black hates an extra word, and revision was always to tighten, never to enlarge. No other Justice but Holmes has been able to pack so much into brief compass, and in Black's case this compass is the product of the sheerest hard work. Usually, toward the end of the year, the Justice would let the clerk try a hand at a first draft of one minor opinion, usually some unimportant dissent.

These rigors have softened a little, but not much. Now the Justice does have the clerks prepare first drafts in from a quarter to a third of the cases, usually the least important ones; but his revisions of those drafts are so complete that they amount to a total rewrite. Today he continues to do the first drafts in the major cases. As ever, he is likely to begin, if the case is substantial, by surrounding himself with everything which has been written on the subject and steeping himself in the details.

Those closest to the Justice find that he shows no flagging of abilities, no lessening of powers with advancing years. He is just as keen at the end of the day or in the evening as he is in the morning. This is perfectly evident from the work itself. As noted, it was in 1963 that the Court overruled *Betts* v. *Brady*. It was in 1963 that the Justice wrote an opinion reviewing the application of the Fourteenth Amendment to business regulations. When Black came to the Court in the days of President Roosevelt's Court-packing plan, a great issue was whether the states could regulate matters of concern to them, and to this the most severe limitation was the due process clause of the Fourteenth Amendment. That limitation has long since withered away. Black's opinion is a tidy review of that whole problem, decisively locking the door on what was a major question of his judicial youth.

In 1963 Black also wrote on whether an airline violated a state antidiscrimination law when it refused to hire a Negro pilot because of his race. The Colorado Supreme Court had held the regulation invalid because the airline was in interstate commerce, and the Court thought this to be an unconstitutional burden on that commerce. The issue was genuinely difficult; it is true that the planes go into many states and that a control by one is therefore necessarily a regulation on commerce in the others. The opinion shows with exceptional clarity why this particular regulation is not an unconstitutional regulation of commerce.

Black's two outstanding qualities remain his single-minded dedication to the Bill of Rights and his almost uncanny instinct for the point, his thrust for the jugular. The law can proliferate so endlessly, its arguments can elaborate so profoundly, that it is possible for even a good mind to wander in the fog. Black's magic is in his capacity to put his finger down swiftly on the precise point on which the case depends, his resistance to all temptations of blind alleys. His instinct is always for what in 1964 he called in one case "the basic principles or common everyday justice." As for his dedication to each American's liberties, it is as Justice Douglas said when Black was seventy, "When the critical account is written, none will be rated higher than Justice Black for consistency in construing the laws and the Constitution so as to protect the civil rights of citizens and aliens whatever the form of repression may be."

This is because he feels civil liberties so deeply. In *Chambers* v. *Florida,* in 1940, the case was murder and the defendants were four Negroes. Subsequent to the murder the police seized some thirty to forty Negroes without warrants for any of them and held them in jail for a protracted period, questioning all of them. What followed is described in Black's opinion:

For five days petitioners were subject to interrogation culminating in Saturday's all night examination. Over a period of five days they steadily refused to confess and disclaimed any guilt. The very circumstances surrounding their confinement and their questioning without any formal charges having been brought, were such as to fill petitioners with terror and frightful misgivings. Some were practical strangers in the community; three were arrested in a one-room farm tenant house which was their home; the haunting fear of mob violence was around them in an atmosphere charged with excitment and public indignation. From virtually the moment of their arrest until their eventual confessions, they never knew when just anyone would be called back to the fourth floor room, and there, surrounded by his accusers and others, interrogated by men who held their very lives— so far as these ignorant petitioners could know—in the balance. The rejection of petitioner Woodward's first "confession," given in the early hours of Sunday morning, because it was found wanting, demonstrates the relentless tenacity which "broke" petitioners' will and rendered them helpless to resist their accusers further.

After a week of constant interrogation, several prisoners confessed. No one knows whether they actually committed the crime— after such a week of grueling, many people would "confess" to almost anything. In holding such confessions inadmissible, Justice Black for a unanimous Court said:

* * * To permit human lives to be forfeited upon confessions thus obtained would make of the constitutional requirement of due process of law a meaningless symbol.
* * * Under our constitutional system, courts stand against any winds that blow as havens of refuge for those who might otherwise suffer because they are helpless, weak, outnumbered, or because they are non-conforming victims of prejudice and public excitement. Due process of law, preserved for all by our Constitution, demands that no such practice as that disclosed by this record shall send any accused to his death. No higher duty, no more solemn responsibility, rests upon this Court, than that of translating into living law and maintaining this constitutional shield deliberately planned and inscribed for the benefit of every human being subject to our Constitution—of whatever race, creed, or persuasion.

Justice Black has dedicated his life to filling that duty.

© Karsh of Ottawa 1964

Chapter Four

MR. JUSTICE

William O. Douglas

THERE IS in the State of Oregon the world's shortest railroad. Set in the center of a recreation area, it consists of a few feet of track running from the edge of a mountain to nowhere at all. On the rock behind it is painted a great black oval for a tunnel and a single caboose gives the appearance either of emerging from or going into it. The name of the line is W.O.D. and D.J.T. Railroad, and its great advantage over a good number of other railroads in the United States is that at least it is not losing any money. President of the line is William O. Douglas.

The Lonesome Road, as it is also called, is considerably more stationary than its president. At any given moment, Bill Douglas may be in his office in the Supreme Court Building in Washington. On the other hand, he may have traveled to some remote corner of the United States to make a speech in behalf of the Israeli cause, by which he sets great store. An inveterate hiker, he may be off in some wilderness area. There has not been such a believer in the genuinely strenuous life in high public office in the United States since Theodore Roosevelt. In 1954, Douglas made a 180-mile hike along the Chesapeake and Ohio Canal to protest the prospect that this old landmark might be turned into a highway. The protest was successful, and each year subsequently, he leads a fifteen-mile hike along a part of the same pathway. The hike has become, in a rather vigorous way, a Washington social event, and last year two hundred hikers went along with him.

There are no territorial limitations on Douglas. The only continent he has not toured is Antarctica, and he may well do that. When the Court is out of session, Douglas is likely to head for some little-known corner of Russia, or a hike in Afghanistan, or a trip into India. These are no luxury tours with the recumbencies of leisurely travel. Douglas covers his miles by jeep or by foot, and his only use for the beaten track is as a point of departure.

Along with this hyperthyroid energy, his endless curiosity, and his passion for the obscurest and highest corners of the outdoors, Douglas is an infinitely productive Supreme Court Justice. His productivity, his interests, his accomplishments on the Bench are immense; but if a man had to stand for eternity on one single act, Douglas might choose a particular dissenting opinion. Douglas succeeded on the Court to the seat which was held by Justice Louis Brandeis. There is in this matter of succession normally no particular significance. Justice Black, for example, succeeded a Justice whose views were almost totally opposite from his own and the judicial inheritance is usually purely sentimental, if even that.

But for Douglas, the inheritance is a very pleasant sentiment because Douglas is in outlook and in skill the closest approximation to Brandeis in the America of the mid-twentieth century. Particularly in matters of individual liberty, in matters of antitrust law, and in problems of business law, Douglas carries on the tradition and the philosophy of his great predecessor.

Never was this more true than in Douglas' dissent in *Dennis* v. *United States*. The great issue was what action, if any, should be taken against the leaders of the American Communist Party. Douglas followed the views expressed by Justice Brandeis a quarter of a century before. That Justice had expounded the principle that speech could be punished in the American tradition only where a serious and immediate injury would be done to the country by allowing the speech to run on. Brandeis had said, and Douglas agreed, that "if there be time to expose through discussion the falsehood and fallacies, to avert the evil by the processes of education, the remedy to be applied is more speech, not enforced silence."

Applying these principles, Douglas turned to the Communists in the United States as they existed in 1951. He listed the works of Marx and Lenin, works in which, as he saw them, "the ugliness of Communism is revealed, its deceit and cunning are exposed, the nature of its activities becomes apparent, and the chances of its success less likely." He then recited his own most basic belief about America:

Full and free discussion has indeed been the first article of our faith. We have founded our political system on it. It has been the safeguard of every religious, political, philosophical, economic, and racial group amongst us. We have counted on it to keep us from embracing what is cheap and false; we have trusted the common sense of our people to choose the doctrine true to our genius and to reject the rest. This has been the one single outstanding tenet that has made our institutions the symbol of freedom and equality. We have deemed it more costly to liberty to suppress a despised minority than to let them vent their spleen.

Douglas accepted the Brandeis view that "when conditions are so critical that there will be no time to avoid the evil that the speech threatens, it is time to call a halt," but he found nothing of the sort in the case before him. "Communism has been so thoroughly exposed in this country that it has been crippled as a political force," he said. "Free speech has destroyed it as an effective political party. It is inconceivable that those who went up and down this country preaching the doctrine of revolution which petitioners espouse would have any success. . . . The doctrine of Soviet revolution is exposed in all of its ugliness and the American people want none of it."

In such circumstances, he believed, the advocacy of domestic Communism presented no clear and present danger. "Some nations less resilient than the United States, where illiteracy is high and where democratic traditions are only budding, might have to take drastic steps and jail these men for merely speaking their creed. But in America they are miserable merchants of unwanted ideas; their wares remain unsold."

59

Douglas declared that "the followers of the creed of Soviet Communism are known to the F.B.I.; that in case of war with Russia they will be picked up overnight as were all prospective saboteurs at the commencement of World War II; that the invisible army of petitioners is the best known, the most beset, and the least thriving of any fifth column in history. Only those held by fear and panic could think otherwise."

Douglas concluded, "Vishinsky wrote in 1938 in *The Law of the Soviet State,* 'in our state, naturally, there is and can be no place for freedom of speech, press, and so on for the foes of socialism.' Our concern," said Douglas, "should be that we accept no such standard for the United States. Our faith should be that our people will never give support to these advocates of revolution, so long as we remain loyal to the purposes for which our Nation was founded."

Douglas has devoted his judicial life to this philosophy.

Whatever the quality of toughness means, Douglas has it. He believes in free speech as the most vital element of the American tradition. But action is something else again. A person may be entitled to speak against the best interests of the United States because other speech should nullify what he says. But anyone who *acts* against the United States is in a wholly different position, and Douglas would unhesitatingly give punishment where punishment is due. The treason case of 1945 is an example. During World War II, a group of German saboteurs were brought to this country by submarine and were landed with explosives and money on the Florida coast. An American citizen named Cramer helped them in various ways, and Cramer was charged with treason. Here was no matter of speech; Cramer's was a plain act against the United States. Yet the Constitution provides that any person charged with the crime of treason may be convicted of this offense only on the testimony of two witnesses to an act of treason. In this case, the witnesses could prove only that the citizen had met with two of the saboteurs in a public restaurant. That meeting could have been perfectly harmless by itself.

Because of the absence of two witnesses to a specific act of treason, a majority of the Court held that Cramer could not be convicted. Justice Douglas dissented in a strong and persuasive opinion. He found the evidence against the citizen "overwhelming," and thought it immaterial that the two saboteurs were old friends of Cramer. "Loyalty to country cannot be subordinated to the amenities of personal friendship," he said. He believes that Cramer did not need to know precisely what the saboteurs were up to; it was enough that he knew that they were up to no good. It was immaterial that the particular act which was observed was by itself harmless, for "the grossest and most dangerous act of treason may be, as in this case, and often is, innocent on its face. Cramer clearly, by his own admission, held the saboteurs' money for them and lied to protect them when he was arrested. To fail to uphold these convictions," he said, was "neither good sense nor good law."

These two cases illustrate Douglas' tolerance of difference of opinion but not of deeds against his country. In each, Douglas was a dissenter. In each, the Court later, in other cases, came close to the position Douglas had taken in the first place.

Another striking similarity of Douglas to Theodore Roosevelt is that each took up exercise as a youngster to recover from illness. As an infant Douglas had infantile paralysis, and when it was over he had to learn to walk again. Climbing in the mountains near Yakima, Washington, in his growing years helped to give strength. His family had come to the Yakima region, with a short stopover in California, while he was still a baby. He was born in Ottertail County, Minnesota, on October 16, 1898. His father, a Presbyterian Church home missionary, died when Douglas was only six, and the family support was left to the enterprise of his mother and the children.

The family financial situation early put Douglas on his own. At an age when Justice Goldberg's father was selling fruit in Chicago, the young Douglas may possibly have been picking it. He earned his way through Whitman College at Walla Walla, Washington, with odd jobs in the winters and full-time employment in the summers. There he continued with some interruption for activity as an Army private in World War I until he graduated in 1920. For two years he taught high school, trying to save enough to go on to law. In 1922, Douglas worked his way to New York to enter the Columbia Law School. He arrived with only a few dollars, worked his way through, and was graduated in 1925.

Three years of practice, two of them with a great New York law firm, followed. He also taught a little law at Columbia and then moved to the Yale Law School in 1928, practicing some law at Yakima, Washington, in the meantime.

Douglas' years at Yale were an exciting time for the law school and a time for great change for America. At school, when he came, Robert Hutchins was Dean. When Hutchins left in 1930 to become President of the University of Chicago, he was succeeded by Charles E. Clark, later a United States Court of Appeals Judge. These were days of great classes and a great faculty when the school went through a period of both genuine intellectual ferment and happy horseplay. In that distinguished group Douglas was himself distinguished, being regarded by his fellow faculty members as very special. Partly this was because he worked incredibly hard. But his work was not of a sort which precluded his share of foolishness.

Douglas was a member of a triumvirate composed of Wesley Sturges, later President of the American Arbitration Association and Dean of the Law School, and Thurman Arnold, later famed both as a trust buster and as a United States Court of Appeals Judge. The years 1930 to 1935 were in the carefree youth of all three, and they became close and constant companions. When Arnold came home from a trip he found a note in his box to tell him to call a certain number and ask for Yvonne, who had met him at a party in San Francisco and wanted to spend more time with him. It was no real surprise to Arnold to have the New Haven morgue answer his eager call and to discover that Douglas had sent the note.

The three had a point system developed by the ingenious Arnold by which each could earn points toward a score which had a nonexistent but immensely valued prize. A mention of one of their works in any court decision was good for one point, a mention in the New Haven papers was good for two points, a mention in the *New York Times* was good for three points, and a picture in the *New York Times* meant the jackpot. Douglas was winning all the honors, so he decided to give the other two a break. One evening when Sturges happened to be speaking to an audience in New Haven and Arnold happened on the same night to be speaking to an audience in Bridgeport, Arnold received a wire as he was about to go on the platform saying "Please mention me in your speech," signed by Wesley Sturges. He dutifully did so without understanding why, only to discover on his return that Sturges had also received a wire signed Thurman Arnold and saying "Please mention me in your speech."

Meanwhile the great depression came to America. Countless Americans lost everything, and many went into bankruptcy. Douglas was a teacher of business law, and for three years he was engaged in special bankruptcy studies. On the Supreme Court he has most frequently been its voice on that subject.

Finally, at the bottom of the depression, Franklin D. Roosevelt was elected President. The debacle of the stock market which had accompanied the depression had revealed great inadequacies in the securities laws of the United States. The exchanges of those days were, as Douglas once put it, nothing but glorified gambling casinos.

A first step of Roosevelt's New Deal was a law creating the Securities and Exchange Commission to deal with stock sales and to regulate the exchanges. Many of the provisions of the Act derived from writings of Justice Brandeis, some dating back to his pre-Supreme Court work. From 1934 to 1936 Douglas was in charge of a special study for the Commission. From 1936 to 1939 he was a member of the Commission, serving the last two years as its chairman.

Douglas' three years at the Commission were among the most turbulent of his life. The early administration had been largely tied up by court orders. When the Supreme Court upheld some of the principal powers of the Commission, it was free to get to work and it did. Effective regulations of stock exchanges began during Douglas' administration. The policy of requiring that the public be given full information about the securities it buys, a policy of full disclosure in which Brandeis had deeply believed, was effectively enforced.

A part of Douglas' accomplishment at the Commission was inducing the exchanges to make some effort for their own self-regulation. It was during this period that Richard Whitney, a former President of the New York Stock Exchange, went to prison for misuse of funds, a condition which was revealed in part as a result of Commission activities. This incident plus Douglas' attitude of encouragement toward self-regulation did encourage the exchanges to take steps to put their own houses in order. During the early period of his service, Douglas was regarded as antibusiness. However, in November, 1938, a speech he made stressing the improvement of the exchanges as a result of their own efforts was thought by the *New York Times* to be "sincerely conciliatory." Douglas had expressly observed in November, 1937, that reforms within the exchanges themselves would permit the SEC to supply only a "police escort" for their activities.

In 1939, President Roosevelt moved Douglas to the Supreme Court. There is no fixed or even traditional geographical requirement for the spread of Supreme Court Justices; they may come from any part of the country. But it seems to most Presidents that as a common-sense matter they ought to be scattered. Applying this standard, it was time for a Westerner, and a likely Western possibility was Senator Lewis Schwellenbach of Washington, who was a good friend of Justice Black, the Roosevelt appointee already on the Court. Douglas was not considered seriously because he was then a resident of Connecticut. However, he had powerful friends in the Senate, including Senators La Follette of Wisconsin and Borah of Idaho. La Follette persuaded Borah to hold a press conference and claim Douglas as a Far Westerner in view of the circumstances that for so large a part of his life, Douglas had been a resident of the State of Washington. Borah did just that, and Roosevelt did choose Douglas. However, his commission as a Justice was necessarily made from a residence in Connecticut.

The Douglas appointment was extremely well received. Conservatives had been frightened at the possibility of Schwellenbach, whom they regarded as a dangerous radical. Douglas was in fact considerably more a liberal than Schwellenbach, but this was not the public image of the two men; such a conservative columnist as Arthur Krock of the *New York Times* responded to Douglas' appointment by saying, "Of the names before Mr. Roosevelt for consideration that of Mr. Douglas was the most reassuring in many ways."

The Senate hearing on the Douglas appointment was perfunctory. The only letter of opposition came from the Prohibition Party, which felt that it deserved a representative on the Supreme Court and therefore opposed all non-prohibitionists on principle. The Senate Committee received a collection of endorsement letters presented by Senator Bone of Washington and within a few minutes approved the nomination. On April 4, 1939, Douglas was confirmed by a vote of sixty-two to four, the dissenters who expressed themselves taking the view that Douglas was a reactionary tool of Wall Street. Rarely has a larger mistake been made than that of the dissenters.

When the Justice was appointed and confirmed, he was the youngest man to have gone to the Supreme Court since Justice Joseph Story, appointed in 1811. Twenty-five years later, we know where the Justice stands on all of the issues which come before the Court. The opinion summary following is almost word for word in his words, lines from his opinions with the quotation marks dropped off for convenience.

The policy of legislation, Douglas believes, its wisdom, its needs, or the appropriateness of the remedy chosen are no matters of judicial concern. Differences of opinion on such matters are for Congress or the states; the Court does not sit as a superlegislature to weigh the wisdom of legislation nor to decide whether a policy which it expresses offends the public welfare.

To make it possible for Congress to legislate, it may—indeed it must—delegate many responsibilities. This the Court will permit, but, where activities or enjoyment, natural and often necessary to the well-being of the American citizen, such as travel, are involved, the Court will construe narrowly all delegated powers that curtail or dilute those privileges. The delegation of the power of Congress must never be unlimited; for the law has reached its finest moments when it has freed man from the unlimited discretion of some ruler, some military official, some bureaucrat. Discretion is a ruthless master, more destructive of freedom than any of man's other inventions.

In approaching his task, the judge must respect precedent without being awed by it. One hesitates to overrule cases, even in the constitutional field, that are of an old vintage; but the Court has always been willing to re-examine and overrule constitutional precedents which history has shown have outlived their usefulness or were conceived in error. The Justice has advocated the overruling of many earlier decisions.

With this free outlook, the Justice is at his best in a case of first impression, one with no precedents to construe or principles previously expounded to apply. He loves to write on a clean slate. But he is not a reckless innovator. He harkens to the lessons of history. Among his predecessors he draws first and oftenest on Brandeis, as in rate making (Mr. Justice Brandeis concurring); antitrust (where the lessons Brandeis taught on the Curse of Bigness have largely been forgotten in high places); on Brandeis the Justice in his classic statements on freedom of speech, and on Brandeis the private citizen. For Douglas, Brandeis' great colleague Justice Holmes is less of a household god.

Douglas likes to learn from English and early American history, whether dealing with a historic civil liberty like the right to trial by jury; or contempt of court; or the long history behind the decision that the law should not be used to pry open one's lips and make him a witness against himself. Of his many books, one which Douglas must have enjoyed doing particularly is *An Almanac of Liberty*. This volume of fragments and readings put together by Douglas is broken into units for each day of the year. In it, Douglas collects all sorts of historical memories such as the trial of Anne Hutchinson in 1637 for heresy or the trial of Sir Walter Raleigh in 1603—or the loyalty case against Dorothy Bailey, which was just as much of an enormity, in 1948.

Yet to Douglas the realities of the situation are more common mentors than the history books. He supports the power of Congress to make broad delegations of authority on the hardheaded practicality that otherwise it cannot perform its functions. When asked whether an airplane can cross through the air over the land of another without thereby committing a trespass, he says of course it can—common sense revolts at the idea that planes can be trespassers. In the antitrust field, choices must be made not on the basis of abstractions but of the realities of modern industrial life. Such practical considerations may occasionally trench even on basic values; for example, to say that the military should have taken the time to weed out the loyal from the disloyal Japanese-Americans at the beginning of World War II would be to assume that the nation could have afforded to take time to do so.

This practical perception is most often used to sustain, not limit, individual rights. Douglas says that the fact that the very thought of a particular procedure is certain to raise havoc with academic freedom is a reason for not permitting it, particularly where youthful indiscretions, mistaken causes, misguided enthusiasms—all long forgotten— will thereby become the ghosts of a harrowing present.

Turning to the right of free speech, Douglas believes that the First Amendment was designed to preclude courts as well as legislators from weighing the values of speech against silence. The First Amendment puts free speech in the preferred position. Freedom of speech can be suppressed only where it is so closely brigaded with illegal action as to be an inseparable part of it. Free speech, free press, free exercise of religion are placed separate and apart; they are above and beyond the police powers; they are not subject to regulation as are the matter of factories, slums, apartment houses, production of oil, and the like.

With regard to other basic rights, Douglas finds the list of those rights of the citizen which are entitled to careful protection a long one. He thinks it not without significance that most of the provisions of the Bill of Rights are procedural. It is procedure that spells much of the difference between rule by law and rule by whim or caprice. He believes that the federal loyalty program violates a host of rights. The loyalty boards decide on evidence which they cannot even appraise. The critical evidence may be the word of an unknown witness who may be a paragon of veracity, a knave, or the village idiot. His name, his reputation, his prejudices, his animosities, his trustworthiness are unknown both to the judge and to the accused. The accused has no opportunity to show that the witness lied or was prejudiced or venal. Without knowing who the accusers are, he has no way of defending.

If one is to be tried for an offense, he has the right of being tried by a jury of both men and women, for the truth is that the two sexes are not fungible; the subtle interplay of influence of one on the other is among the imponderables. As for other rights, Douglas believes as strongly as Black and has stood with Black for more than twenty years in the belief that a defendant who may be innocent desperately needs a lawyer to help extricate him from a charge. He also believes that in protecting against unlawful searches and seizures, the courts should throw their weight on the side of the citizen and against the lawless police.

Douglas recognizes other less conventional but equally basic rights. He regards the right of privacy as one of the unique values of our civilization. Liberty as used in the Fifth Amendment must include privacy as well as the more conventional rights if it is to be a repository of freedom. Also important is the right to work, the most precious liberty that man possesses. Man has as much right to work as he has to live, to be free, to own property. Immediately connected with both of these—that is, the right to be let alone and the right to work—is the right to be free of wrongful deportation, for deportation visits a great hardship on the individual, depriving him of the right to stay and live and work in this land of freedom. Douglas is the great traveler of the

Court, and he believes that the right to travel is a part of the "liberty" of which the citizen cannot be deprived without due process of law. Freedom of movement across frontiers in either direction, as well as inside frontiers, is part of our heritage.

Douglas believes not only in individual liberty but in economic liberty, and to him economic liberty requires free competition. He is against having little, independent units gobbled up by bigger ones. Such power as that of the United States Steel Company, for example, can be benign, or it can be dangerous; he believes it should not exist. Certainly a company as big as that, with its tremendous leverage on the economy, is big enough. In April of 1964, he had the immense satisfaction of writing for the Court an opinion which adopted what had been dissenting views of his own a decade earlier in one of the steel antitrust cases. He thinks it bad for the country to allow independent businesses to be swallowed up by absentee owners. There follows a serious loss of citizenship. He who is a leader in the village becomes dependent on outsiders for his action and policy. Clerks responsible to a superior in a distant place take the place of resident proprietors beholden to no one. And so wherever he can, Douglas would interpret the antitrust laws in favor of the maintenance of free enterprise. This is particularly true in the patent field, where he would harmonize the statutes as closely as possible with the policy of the antitrust laws.

The most striking quality of Douglas is his restless brilliance. As a boy, he was the top student at his high school and he won a scholarship to his college. He was graduated from his college with Phi Beta Kappa and honors. He was second in his class at law school. He quickly became one of the youngest and probably one of the highest-paid professors of law in the United States. He was a young and splendidly successful Securities and Exchange Commissioner; he was one of the youngest Justices ever to come to the Court.

On the Court, Douglas has been one of the tremendous workhorses. In the early part of his service, when the Court handled more cases, he was comfortably capable of turning out thirty majority opinions of uniformly high quality each year. He uses his law clerks probably less than other Justices. He writes the first draft of his opinions in longhand and these are not likely to be much changed by the time they are printed for circulation to the other Justices. He can never be comfortable until his work is behind him, and when the Chief Justice assigns him an opinion it is very likely to be finished within the week. Probably no one but Justice Holmes in this century has worked so fast.

Fast can mean good-fast or careless-fast. With Douglas it is the former. Moreover he is no mere specialist within the Court; he plays the entire field. Colorful opinions in civil liberties fields have been mentioned; but the work of the Supreme Court is more than a constant seminar on the rights of the American people. There is plain hard work to be done on matters of taxation, matters of business reorganization and bankruptcies, matters of public acquisition of lands, truly difficult and technical questions of what law is to be applied in many situations. In all these, Douglas has made major contributions, and in some of them he has been virtually indispensable to the Court for many of his years of service.

The speed of Douglas gives him time for a wholly separate career as a traveler and as a writer. He has turned out twenty books since he has been on the Court. Other Justices over the years have done little outside writing; that other young Justice, Joseph Story, in the first part of the nineteenth century did a good deal. But no one has ever approached anything like the Douglas output. Indeed, there is scarcely a full-time professional author in the United States who can compare with him.

Some of these are travel books. *Strange Lands and Friendly People, Beyond the High Himalayas,* and *Russian Journey* are examples. Some deal with the American West, such as *My Wilderness,* the *Pacific West,* or *Muir of the Mountain.* Others deal with political philosophy or history, such as *The Right of the People* or *Mr. Lincoln and the Negroes.*

The most remarkable feature of the Douglas work, in court and out, is its incredible range. This is the man who truly knows more about more different things than any other public figure in America. His interests are well described in a description by a former clerk:

The buzzer for me from the Justice's Chamber, or the note from the bench or conference, would usually mean that I was asked to find a particular citation or, perhaps, to write a memorandum on some narrow point of law. But, at times, I might be asked to ascertain the height of a Himalayan Peak, the reign of a Roman emperor, or whether the Pennsylvania Constitution of 1776 had been ratified. The breadth of the man was best illustrated to me by our occasional talks, particularly on Saturday when we would have lunch across the street from the Court Building. During the walk over, he might stop and chat with the gardener about the most efficient method to maintain the shrubbery about the building. He might point out to me some obscure plant, name it and comment that it was an excellent representative of its species. At lunch we might discuss a legal point involved in a pending case or incidents in the Court's recent history. But the discussion would often range much further than the work of the Court —from the art of hiking and the necessity of preserving wilderness areas inviolate to the problems of land reform in Pakistan, American foreign policy and the current Presidential campaign. He would speak with informed authority about the flora of Iran (of which he has presented a personal collection to the National Herbarium in Washington), as well as the intricacies of corporate finance.

The Douglas opinions benefit from his writing experience, for as the only regularly best-selling author ever to sit in the Supreme Court, he gives to his judicial work much of the same flair which he displays in the bookstalls. This includes the power to emphasize with brevity as in the *Steel* case where he said, "Today a kindly President uses the seizure power to effect a wage increase and to keep the steel furnaces in production. Yet tomorrow another President might use the same power to prevent a wage increase, to curb trade unions, to regiment labor as oppressively as industry thinks it has been regimented by this seizure."

Douglas often makes his point with a single sentence. Referring to community standards as a test of obscenity, he said, "It creates a regime wherein the battle between the literati and the Philistines, the Philistines are certain to win." Or, speaking of the exclusion of a doctor from the practice of his profession in New York, "When a doctor cannot save lives in America because he is opposed to Franco in Spain, it is time to call a halt and look critically at the neurosis that has possessed us."

Douglas can make his point vividly, as for example where a confession was obtained from a fifteen-year-old Negro boy after an all-night interrogation. Douglas observed, "Age fifteen is a tender and difficult age for a boy of any race. He cannot be judged by the more exacting standards of maturity. That which would leave a man cold and unimpressed can overwhelm a lad in his early teens. This is a period of great instability which the crisis of adolescence produces. Mature men might possibly stand the ordeal from midnight to 5:00 A.M. But we cannot believe that a lad of tender years is a match for the police in such a contest. He needs counsel and support if he is not to become the victim first of fear, then of panic."

The brilliance and the speed of Douglas are both a blessing and a curse because sometimes they make him restless. At times there appears to be *no* scene large enough to give play to all his energy. Hence there are sporadic suggestions that he may sometime leave the job to do something else. In 1944, President Roosevelt gave the Democratic Convention its choice of Harry Truman or Douglas as Vice Presidential candidates; had the Convention made the other choice, presumably even Douglas would have been busy enough. There have been occasional stories that he might leave the Court to become Secretary of the Interior (this because of his love for and intimate knowledge of the West) or Secretary of State (because of his prodigious knowledge of international relations) or something else. All this talk is a gossipy by-product of the extraordinary breadth of the Justice's interests. He is interested in the problems of the Interior and he does have deep-felt beliefs, which he occasionally expresses, about parks and

wilderness. He does feel freer than many of the other Justices to discuss non-legal matters, and particularly those relating to international
relations; he does learn on his trips, and this experience he wants to
contribute. But the fact that Douglas maintains more interests than
one is no abandonment of his primary love for the law. It does mean
that he sees America whole, and is not satisfied to see the country fall
short of the perfection to which he thinks it can rise.

Douglas is alarmed because he sees his fellow countrymen smug,
complacent, and drifting. He sees a school system which he thinks inadequate, with underpaid teachers. "Research on disease lags. Slum
clearance and urban developments suffer. While our population is
burgeoning, our recreational facilities are inadequate and little is
being done about them. We are reducing year by year our wilderness
areas and making cesspools out of our rivers. We are far behind the
Russians in exploring space. Their rate of growth is much greater
than ours. We have indeed no national growth policy. Yet unless we
launch one we will never be able to handle continuously the great expenditures for military purposes and the increasing amounts needed
for social and educational ends," he has said.

In Douglas' mind, these conditions cannot be separated from the
law. He finds complacency, mediocrity, and intolerance the greatest
enemies of the country, and he finds legal institutions fostering all three
of these. From the day Douglas hopped a freight train heading for the
Columbia Law School, and even before, he has never been a conform-
ist. Douglas feels that legal actions such as loyalty programs put a
premium on conformity, causing men to believe that they can get
ahead in the world only by being as much like everyone else as possible.
But the world's progress is not made by so many lookalikes; it depends
on the brilliant individual who can find a new way. This is the man
who can have the "flash of genius" (a phrase Douglas has used in the
field of industrial patents) necessary to spark progress. Douglas is
against a legal system which makes that kind of progress impossible by
extolling conformity and thereby promoting the mediocre.

73

Twenty-five years of experience show Douglas as thoroughly competent in his work, and by no means approaching the point of slackening productivity at which retirement should be, or is likely to be, considered. For year in, year out competence he stands at the top among any Justices, past or present; not only in views but in stature he is fairly comparable to Brandeis.

The opinions of 1963–1964 show him hard and typically at his work. One was an election case involving the method of nominating the United States Senator and Governor, as well as other statewide officers in Georgia. Under the Georgia law, as it was when this suit was filed, 938 people in the smallest county had as much influence on the result as 92,721 people in the largest county. A single resident of the smallest county had ninety-nine times the voting power of a resident of the largest. While the suit was pending the law changed, but not by enough to change the principle of the discrimination; the residents of the smaller counties still had a greatly disproportionate influence in the choice of a Governor and a Senator.

Douglas wrote the opinion of the Court holding this system unconstitutional. The resultant opinion is brisk, workmanlike, decisive, and clear. It runs a dozen pages, the first of which state the facts, clearly and distinctly. The next few paragraphs dispose of important technical jurisdictional questions as to court procedures in cases of this kind. Then comes the argument, which is written with such extraordinary simplicity that a bright child could easily follow it; and yet this is the simplicity which conceals art for it uses all the proper legal building blocks to make a sound structure. Douglas observes that no state can abridge the right of a Negro or of a woman to vote, so that "if a state in a statewide election weighed the male vote more heavily than the female vote, or the white vote more heavily than the Negro vote, none could successfully contend that that discrimination was allowable."

If this is so, he continued, how can one person be given twice or ten times the voting power of another person in a statewide election merely because he lives in a rural area or because he lives in the smallest rural county? Reviewing other decisions, Douglas shows that every voter is entitled to vote and that every voter is entitled to have his vote correctly counted and reported. The underlying principle of this must be "that every voter is equal to every other voter in his state. . . . The conception of political equality from the Declaration of Independence to Lincoln's Gettysburg Address to the Fifteenth, Seventeenth, and Nineteenth Amendments can mean only one thing—one person, one vote." Nor will equality of numbers alone satisfy him; in a 1964 dissent he objected to the apparent Manhattan Island practice of having fairly equal numbers in the four Congressional districts but of drawing the boundaries so as to put almost all the Negroes and Puerto Ricans into a single district.

This essay began by quoting from an expression of Douglas on individual liberty in 1951 and may conclude with his return to that theme and his re-expression of the same Brandeis belief in 1963. In one 1963 case, the issue was whether Florida could require the local chapter of the National Association for the Advancement of Colored People to turn over its membership lists to a state legislative investigating committee. The opinion of the Court held that, on the facts of this particular case, these records need not be revealed. Justice Douglas agreed in a separate opinion.

Douglas began by restating his faith that as part of the American way of life, people must be allowed to be different. One way to permit difference is to permit people to gather together in small groups, as the NAACP did in Florida; as Douglas sees it, this freedom of association for lawful purposes is a right of the citizen protected by the First Amendment. The freedom of association, he believes, is a part of the freedom of assembly which is expressly protected in the Constitution and which underlies the insatiable American desire to gather together in organizations. These endless organizations are not much subject to investigation because the legislature could not legally pass laws about them, and therefore there is nothing proper to investigate.

Much depends, says Douglas, upon protecting the right of privacy of the individual, a right which was given its start in American law by Brandeis in the 1890's. As always, Douglas sees the matter practically: "Unpopular groups, like popular ones, are protected. Unpopular ones, if forced to disclose their membership lists may suffer reprisals or other forms of public hostility. But whether a group is popular or unpopular, the right of privacy implicit in the First Amendment creates an area into which the government may not enter."

This is true because "the views the citizen entertains, the beliefs he harbors, the utterances he makes, the ideology he embraces and the people he associates with are no concern of government." If an organization were engaged in some criminal conduct, then it could be prosecuted and its members could be investigated. But there was no suggestion of anything criminal about any of the activities of the NAACP. The possibility that it may have some members who have committed crimes is immaterial; "one man's privacy may not be invaded because of another's perversity."

Referring to Orwell's frightful anticipation of life in a totalitarian state in 1984, when a head of state called Big Brother would punish not merely the deeds or the words but also the thoughts of any citizen, Douglas concluded, "Where government is the Big Brother, privacy gives way to surveillance. But our commitment is otherwise. By the First Amendment we have staked our security on freedom to promote a multiplicity of ideas, to associate at will with kindred spirits, and to defy governmental intrusion into these precincts."

For twenty-five years, William O. Douglas has stood on the ramparts in defense of the liberties of the individual American citizen. He has had his successes and his failures; these have been hard years. But if the symbolic 1984 never comes, and if Big Brother never does get his grip on the throat of every American citizen, no person will deserve more credit for the resistance than William O. Douglas.

Chapter Five

MR. JUSTICE
Tom C. Clark

TOM CLARK is the traveling salesman of justice, and he clocks more miles in this cause each year than all of the rest of the Supreme Court put together. When he gets five pounds over the weight he allows himself, he points to the small abdominal protuberance which results and says, mournfully, "Banquet food." He has beyond doubt eaten more chicken, shaken more hands, and sat through more introductions in any given year than even his good friend and fellow Texan, President Lyndon Johnson.

The total is a statistical spectacular. In 1962 and 1963 he spoke to well over two-thirds of the state trial judges of the United States, and there are some 2,800 of them. Judge-training programs which he superintends and which he joins whenever possible, have been held in thirty-seven states, and all fifty states will have been reached in 1964. He declines twenty-five to fifty invitations a week from all over the country; but he particularly tries to accept those from the less populous areas. "Nobody pays enough attention to them," he says in his mild way.

Clark is likely to turn up wherever lawyers and judges, or Boy Scouts, or a Masonic breakfast—at one of which he recently spoke to over 12,000 Masons—or his legal fraternity, or almost any kind of Texans, need him. It would be hard to rate his loyalties in any absolute order—perhaps the Texans do come first—but as Attorney General of the United States he came to be sharply aware of juvenile crime; and so the Boy Scouts get a surprising amount of attention from this Supreme Court Justice. His greatest on-tour accomplishment has been solid progress in the improved administration of justice and greater good will toward his own Court.

And yet, to all this he gives only his spare time. First and foremost, Clark is a Justice of the Court, carrying the full weight of its duties as his prime task, and treating his missionary activities as incidental good works. From what is really a terrible outside load, his Court work is never allowed to suffer. The plain physical burden for a man well into his sixties is severe. His hard week in Court ends with an intensive conference on Friday with the other Justices. Clark has been known to go from the conference room to the airport, meet with a Bar group in California on Saturday, fly back on Sunday, and be in his seat on the Bench again on Monday morning.

For some years, when the Court met at noon, Clark exercised by walking to the courthouse with Chief Justice Warren. But when the Court shifted its meeting hour to 10:00 A.M.—a move sparked by Clark because he thought more could be accomplished by an earlier start—the walk had to go. He now tries to keep fit by regular use of the Court's small exercise room, and may visit unselfconsciously with a friend while riding an Exercycle or perspiring his way to health in a hotbox. His friends worry over whether any one man should attempt so much, but Clark, though he sometimes appears to be dead tired, seems indestructible.

Although contemporary articles concerning Clark's life emphasize his political talents, the fact is that he never ran for political office and never received appointment by reason of any political activity. His judicial service illustrates that his decisions are remarkably free of personal or political motivations. One of his most difficult votes must have been to declare illegal President Harry Truman's seizure of the steel plants. Clark had been Truman's Attorney General, Truman had appointed him to the Supreme Court, and the Justice was personally devoted to the President. He knew how much vindication meant in that difficult moment to Truman. But he believed that the seizure was illegal, and he said so. The respect Clark felt for President Truman shines through the opinion, but, borrowing a phrase from an earlier Justice, he concluded that it was his duty to disagree no matter how much his opinion might "differ from that of very great authorities."

Again, in the difficult school-prayer cases, Clark is a truly religious man who knew that he could be a hero to many by voting that school prayers were constitutional. He nonetheless wrote his absolutely decisive conviction that they were illegal.

And yet in a larger, and very proper sense, Clark uses his highly schooled public relations talent on the Court. After the first school-prayer case, in 1962, the Court was ferociously attacked for its alleged atheism. Clark, feeling that the country, once it truly understood the issue, would largely agree with the Court, soon made a tactful speech on the public misunderstanding of the opinion. Appearing before the Commonwealth Club of San Francisco, he spoke publicly about a Court decision for what is probably the only time in his judicial life. The speech was quoted all over America, particularly for Clark's stress on the widespread misinformation which resulted from the circumstance that the opinion was handed down as one of a group of fifteen decisions on a busy Monday. Newspaper people, said Clark, had no opportunity to read what they were writing about and so greatly exaggerated the decision. (A Columbia School of Journalism thesis was soon written demonstrating his point.) The next school-prayer decision, in 1963, Clark wrote himself. It closely followed the first, yielding no ground at all; but Clark wrote with such persuasive reasonableness that the decision has been almost universally accepted.

The same flair shows in Clark's dealing with his fellow Justices. He knows that it takes five to make a majority and that unanimity is always desirable. Where he can conciliate another Justice's point of view by yielding a point, without surrendering his own convictions, he does. This is the negotiating skill of long practice.

Clark was introduced to the law by his father, who practiced in

Dallas for over half a century. He was born in Dallas, Texas, on September 23, 1899. In 1917 and 1918 he attended the Virginia Military Institute, and then proceeded to the United States Army Infantry. After the war he finished his college and law school work at the University of Texas, getting his law degree in 1922. From 1922 to 1927 he practiced in Dallas with his father's firm. Then he took his first public post, civil district attorney for Dallas County, an appointive job of the commissioners of the county. As civil district attorney, Clark handled the general run of the legal housekeeping of Dallas County. He had the land condemnations, tax suits, money claims, juvenile problems, and similar matters. The job permitted him also to engage in private practice from his office in the County Records Building across the street from the courthouse. He was in the courts every day, giving him a general trial experience, as well as access to townspeople making up the jury panels, acquaintanceship with lawyers, and appearances as the county's lawyer before all of the judges.

This latter experience proved rewarding, for one of the judges before whom he often appeared gave Clark his first big break by appointing him as Special Master in the *Joiner Oil* case. Joiner had been the developer of one of the first wells of the east Texas field. Before he struck oil, the financial as well as the geological going had been tough; and Joiner had financed himself by giving out certificates of interest in his holding. These he distributed like checks, using them for purchases of equipment, payment of labor, and purchase of supplies. As hopes rose, the certificates became negotiable (at a discount, usually), their holders using them to pay for other goods and services.

Then the well hit, and a unit of interest became worth about $1,800. There were hundreds in circulation, some valid, some forged, some which were in the hands of persons not entitled to them, others unenforceable for one legal reason or another. A Dallas court got the job of administering the payout, and Clark was appointed as Special Master to handle the job for the judge. He took evidence, heard witnesses, decided as to all of the certificates—and in two depression years earned a large fee for his time, in addition to carrying on as civil district attorney and with other work.

In 1933, Clark had finished the Joiner assignment and left the civil district attorney job to begin a partnership with William McCraw, the district attorney in charge of criminal cases of Dallas County, an elective position. "McCraw," he has said, "was the greatest natural politician Texas ever saw except Lyndon Johnson." These two young men set out on the simple business of making a living and of electing McCraw as Governor of Texas.

The two men made a fine start, but McCraw could not wait. In 1934 he ran for the office of Texas attorney general, though Clark counseled discreet delay. The opposition, two attorneys far better known than McCraw, was rough; but McCraw covered the state with Clark's help and was elected. In 1935, therefore, Clark was without a partner; but he hired a couple of younger men to help him. Being the ex-partner of the attorney general did not hurt his practice, and in 1935 and 1936 he did extremely well financially. McCraw failed to be elected Governor but later was a district judge of Dallas County until his death in 1955.

Clark was still a country boy, and he had a good deal to learn about big-city ways, and particularly about big-city titles. After Franklin D. Roosevelt's overwhelming re-election in 1936, Senator Tom Connally of Texas, a warm friend of the Clark family, boosted Clark for the position of Assistant Attorney General in the United States Department of Justice. Next to the Attorney General, these posts are the highest posts of the Department. In January, 1937, Clark received a wire from the Senator that he had been appointed Assistant Attorney General in the new Roosevelt Administration.

Clark shut his office and headed for Washington. He arrived the day after President Roosevelt sent Congress his plan to add six new Justices to the Supreme Court, and reported for work. He was re-

ceived immediately as a Connally man, because Connally was Chairman of the Foreign Relations Committee. The Senator was essential
to the President's purpose, but was clearly doubtful about it; and
Clark was forthwith asked to approach Connally. This Clark declined,
on the ground of its inappropriateness.

There remained the matter of Clark's own appointment. It quickly
turned out that he was not to be Assistant Attorney General at all. He
was to be an assistant *to* the Attorney General. What was offered to
him was a run-of-the-mine job at a run-of-the-mine salary.

Clark's problem was whether to stay or to go home, dust off the
shingle, and return to his practice. He decided to give the Department
a try, and has been either with the Department of Justice or on the
Supreme Court ever since.

Clark's first job was in the "graveyard" of the Department, the
War Risk Litigation Section. It was busily engaged, in the exciting
year 1937, in cleaning up claims left over from World War I. But
when President Roosevelt and the Department of Justice in the Court
Reform bill took the position that the Supreme Court was not doing
its work, Chief Justice Hughes passed the word to the District Judges
to dispose of all old litigation which put the prod to the Department
of Justice on the war-risk cases. Suddenly hundreds of torpid cases
came to life, and Clark got his first taste of the Department as he
moved about the country defending against these claims.

Clark was fortunate in these cases, never losing a single one. This
gained notice in the Department and gave him a cordial relationship
with the higher-ups, including Joseph B. Keenan, the assistant to the
Attorney General. When Attorney General Cummings decided to
retire, there was a vacancy at the top; and Mr. Keenan was an as-
pirant to the highest chair. Clark backed Keenan enthusiastically.
FDR had other ideas, and instead chose Frank Murphy of Michigan;
but Clark had in Keenan a friend near the top who was indebted to
him. Keenan asked Clark what division of the Department he wished

to work in, and Clark chose Antitrust. With that election, his career was moving in earnest.

Head of the Antitrust Division in those days was Thurman Arnold, trust buster extraordinary. Arnold, who had a background of a practicing country lawyer as well as having been a Yale Law School professor, recognized in Clark a talent he could use, and, after a period in which Clark was enforcing the Wage-Hour law, Arnold sent him to New Orleans to try the antitrust phases of the Huey Long debacle. Vast scandals had been exposed in Louisiana, and most of them were within the province of the Criminal Division of the Department of Justice; but among the other peccadillos of those days in New Orleans was a combination of contractors to rig the bids on public works. Among other lucrative arrangements, they had provided that the successful bidder should pay a certain amount of his fee to all the other, unsuccessful bidders. This involved an illegal combination, and was within Antitrust jurisdiction.

Clark sent his wife home to Dallas and settled down for six months in the French Quarter of New Orleans. He filed some two dozen indictments and got pleas of guilty on them all. Then he returned to Washington, reopened his home, and discovered that Arnold wanted him to take over the West Coast operations of Antitrust.

It was an opportunity and a blow because the Clarks were settled again; but "Mary was always a good soldier," Clark remembers, and off they went to California. His first move was to bring about a settlement of a case involving several large oil companies, and he quickly moved in to wind up in sixty days a case which had been the full-time job of a crew of lawyers and secretaries for two years. Clark handled the case against the West Coast Lumbermen's Association, that of the *Southern California Grocers* case, and was in the midst of the trial of the *Lumber Products* case in San Francisco when Pearl Harbor Day came. The West Coast population immediately became alarmed at the Japanese scattered among them. Clark, in retrospect, thinks the

8 3

scare was utterly baseless, and fears that much of it was motivated by plain envy and greed for the Japanese truck gardens. But however irrational the fear seems now, it was very real then; and Clark suddenly found himself appointed as Civilian Coordinator to the Western Defense Command by President Roosevelt. His principal client was General De Witt and the principal legal duty became first, a curfew for all enemy aliens, including the Japanese, and finally, the movement of the latter to camps inland.

The transfer of the Japanese—most of them were American citizens—on purely racial grounds was one of the cruelest and worst days in American constitutional history; there was scarcely a moment since Washington's time in which a great people has fallen so far short of its own aspirations. The Japanese-Americans, who proved to be largely innocent, were taken from their homes and their properties to be confined for years in interior America. The act may have been legal but it is scarcely a tribute to the free and the brave.

Nonetheless, Clark was no policymaker; these orders came from Washington, and it was simply his job to help carry them out. It is a tribute to the Western Defense Command and later to the War Relocation Authority which succeeded it that the job was done about as well as it could be done; a cruel program was not compounded with unnecessary cruelties. The unforgivable never became the savage. For this, Clark, among many others, deserves credit. He helped find places for the camps, arrange legal details of their installations, and at one point was very nearly shot by an angry mob in Colorado which did not want the Japanese coming to them any more than the Californians wished them to stay where they were. He argued the legality of the curfew regulations, his position later being upheld by the Supreme Court.

Then, later in 1942, he was brought back to Washington where he has been ever since. Thurman Arnold believed that everything relating to business belonged in the Antitrust Division and so, for no better reason than this, the War Frauds Unit of World War II was placed there with Clark at its head. With the Government suddenly spending money on military procurement, there were bound to be those who would find the great flow of funds an invitation to swindle. The United States Senate had several years before set up a committee headed by Senator Harry Truman. Its investigations uncovered many frauds against the Government which were referred by the Senator to the War Frauds Unit of the Department. It was the beginning of the most important experience of Clark's life. The Senator and the prosecutor hit it off.

The War Frauds section was busy with the Committee references and the F.B.I. investigations. It eventually handled some seven thousand complaints and returned about a thousand indictments. In the three years following Clark's appointment, hundreds of trials were conducted with more than four hundred pleas of guilty and more than one hundred convictions. The offenses ran from deliberate production of defective war materials to bribery of Government personnel. One colonel was convicted for accepting bribes, and many large corporations were defendants.

In 1943 and 1944, Clark gained important promotions. When Arnold was appointed judge, he steered Clark in as his own successor as head of the Antitrust Division. At last Clark was an Assistant Attorney General in fact. A little later, Attorney General Biddle moved many of the functions of the Antitrust Division (including War Frauds) over to the Criminal Division and put Clark in charge of it instead of Antitrust. It was during this period that Clark argued and won his first case before the Supreme Court.

He also prosecuted, in December, 1944, the spy case of *United States* v. *Colepaugh and Gimple* before a Special Military Court empaneled by President Roosevelt. The court found them both guilty and assessed the death penalty.

In 1944, Clark and his friend Senator Truman supported House

Speaker Sam Rayburn of Texas for the Vice Presidential nomination at the time of President Roosevelt's nomination for his fourth term. But Rayburn had opposition at home in his primary election to the House of Representatives which kept him from the convention, and the Texas delegation proved surprisingly lukewarm to what should have been its favorite son. Finally Rayburn told Clark and Truman he was withdrawing from consideration and suggested that Truman himself be a candidate. This was not the first time that this suggestion was made, but it caught on quickly thereafter; and the upshot was President Roosevelt's letter to the Convention, written from his special train, stating that he would take either Truman or William O. Douglas, then on the Supreme Court.

Clark had nothing personally to do with the letter, but he did have a hand in the events which followed. Within a year of the Convention, President Roosevelt had been re-elected and had died; Truman was President, and Tom Clark was Attorney General of the United States.

Clark succeeded Francis Biddle, Roosevelt's wartime Attorney General. These were shoes hard to fill, but Clark set out to try. He was the first man to work himself up from the lowest ranks of a departmental attorney to the office of the Attorney General.

As a career man, Clark wanted to bring the office closer to the employees. His first act in this regard was to choose to take his oath of office before the Washington staff of the Department in the Great Hall of the Justice Building rather than at the White House. In a short talk at that time he pledged an "open door" policy toward all staff members, set up a "Suggestion Box" outside of his office to receive suggestions from his co-workers, and sent a personal note to every employee inviting suggestions for improving staff work. In quick succession, after the war's end in 1945, he set up the Attorney General's Committee on Juvenile Delinquency to combat juvenile crime, which has now been expanded by Congressional action. He organized the

National Conference on Citizenship to spotlight attention on the duties and responsibilities of the citizen. Later this organization was granted a Congressional Charter under the same name and continues to be active. Believing that the people of the nation needed an after-the-war stimulus to their American heritage, he sponsored the Freedom Train which toured the nation for two years exhibiting the original historic documents pertaining to American freedom, such as the Declaration of Independence, the Constitution, the Bill of Rights, and hundreds of others.

However, Clark personally carried on the most important function of his office, counseling the President of the United States, and personally argued three cases before the United States Supreme Court, many more than is usual for an Attorney General. Each was important and each he won. The first was the *United Mine Workers'* case, involving the coal strike of 1946. President Truman, on Clark's advice, seized the coal mines, and John L. Lewis and his mine workers continued their strike despite an injunction. A trial court fined both Lewis and the union very substantially, and the Supreme Court upheld the result. Second was *United States* v. *California,* a case establishing the jurisdiction of the United States over the rich oil lands off the Pacific Coast. To sustain this position Clark had to go flatly against the interest of the State of Texas, for he made clear that the same rule would apply to all offshore oil. Third was the *Paramount Pictures* case, a major antitrust matter.

When Justice Frank Murphy died in 1949, President Truman promptly called Clark to the White House to tell him that he wished to appoint him in Murphy's place. Clark was not surprised because President Truman had once suggested to him that in picking his Number Two man Clark should "be sure to select one that can succeed you, because I may want you somewhere else." But Clark did demur politely, saying, "What's the matter, aren't you satisfied with me as Attorney General?" The President assured Clark that he was perfectly well satisfied but that he did feel that Clark could do a useful job at the Court.

The appointment was not confirmed without some contest. Senators Connally and Lyndon Johnson of Texas warmly endorsed him. Johnson told a committee that "it is a wise appointment, and I think he is an able and fair man." Texans by the hundreds sent in their endorsements; the printed record contains thirty-five or more pages of their applause.

But the enthusiasm was by no means unanimous. The *New York Herald Tribune* thought that as Attorney General Clark had been a failure. The *Washington Post* thought him unsuitable. Professor Fowler Harper of the Yale Law School, appearing for the National Lawyers' Guild, charged that Clark was responsible for the deficiencies of the loyalty program and charged that he was insensitive to civil liberties. Elizabeth Gurley Flynn, appearing for the Communist Party of the United States, charged that the appointment was an affront to Negroes, to labor, and to all who believed in the Bill of Rights. The *Chicago Tribune* believed that "Mr. Truman disgraced himself when he proposed Tom Clark for the Supreme Court," and added that there must be at least "50,000 lawyers in the United States who know more law than Clark does or ever will." The thirty-five pages of endorsements were, in short, balanced with another thirty-five pages of condemnations.

The attacks on Clark centered on four main points. The first was the charge that he would be a Red-baiting extremist, insensitive to rights of free speech and free association. The second was that he would be hostile to Negroes. The third was that he would be indifferent to the rights of persons accused of crime, tolerating or even approving of bullying law-enforcement practices. Finally, there was the charge that Clark was simply incompetent and would be unable to tend to the judicial business.

On free-speech matters, Clark's philosophy has not been that of

Holmes or Brandeis, nor Black or Douglas; indeed he has probably disagreed with the latter two Justices in three-quarters of the serious free-speech and related matters before the Court in the past fifteen years. Undoubtedly Clark has been deeply concerned about internal security. In the case of a conflict between internal security on the one hand, and individual freedom on the other, he tips the scales in favor of what he believes to be necessary to his country's security; but there has certainly been nothing of extremism in his stand.

Far from being a Red-baiter he has taken a middle course. He has voted to uphold the principal congressionally imposed anti-Communist restrictions and he has voted to uphold the principal federal loyalty program cases which have come before the Court. On the other hand he has been by no means insensitive to the abuses of such programs. In 1952, his opinion held unconstitutional the Oklahoma loyalty oath, because under it a person could be guilty without knowing the character of the organization he might have joined. In invalidating this statute, Clark said: "There can be no dispute about the consequences visited upon a person excluded from public employment on disloyalty grounds. In the view of the community, the stain is a deep one; indeed, it has become a badge of infamy." Moreover, he stood up strongly against discharging persons solely on the ground that they had claimed their Fifth Amendment privileges in the course of a legislative investigation. He declared that the privilege of a citizen not to testify against himself is one of his most valuable rights, and one which would be reduced to nothing if its exercise were construed to be a plea of guilty. In another area of freedom of speech, it was his opinion which determined that motion pictures were a kind of "speech" and therefore entitled to appropriate protection under the First Amendment, a decision which required the overruling of a 1915 case.

There was no basis for the charge that Clark was unsympathetic to Negro rights when he was appointed, and experience has proved this allegation to have no foundation at all. He has been with the

8 9

majority in substantially every case upholding Negro rights for his entire fifteen years on the Bench. His 1964 opinion holding unconstitutional a Louisiana statute requiring that the race of each candidate be printed on the ballot is a model of concise workmanship.

The charge that Clark would prove to be prosecutor on the Bench, a kind of a hanging judge, loading all the procedural dice against the defendants, has likewise proved to be absolutely baseless. Clark is unquestionably sympathetic to the problems of prosecuting attorneys, whose problems he well knows. In one conspicuous instance, a matter of the right of the defendant to see certain documents in the possession of the prosecution, his strenuous objection to revealing the documents sparked the passage by the Congress of the so-called "Jencks Act." But he has certainly exhibited a thorough sympathy for the rights of the defendant as well. He joined the majority of the Court in the landmark decision holding that no person in any court, state or federal, may be deprived of counsel in a criminal case simply because of his poverty. He wrote for the Court its trailblazing opinion, overruling an earlier decision, holding that evidence obtained by illegal seizure by state police authorities could not be used at trial. Outside the Court as a leader of public opinion and of the Bar, he has taken a strong stand in boosting better defense practices for all.

As for his competence, Clark's fifteen years on the Court break into three roughly equal periods. The pattern of the entire fifteen years has been a curve of constant growth. When he first came to the Court he was wholly inexperienced in judicial work, and had for a long time been a legal executive with a large staff. Clark often tells the story that he asked Mr. Justice Jackson, also a former Attorney General, how long it took him to get acclimated on the Court. Jackson replied that he had asked Chief Justice Hughes the same question and the Chief had told him "about three years," to which Jackson added, "It took me nearer five." In Clark's second year, he wrote really important opinions on problems of state taxation of interstate business

90

which brought more light to that complicated area than it had seen in some time. And he has since added additional opinions in this field of the highest quality, lending clarity and substance to the law.

By the beginning of his second five years, Clark had firmly taken hold of his work. Both Chief Justice Vinson and Justice Jackson had died and Warren and Harlan had succeeded them. Clark's work became more penetrating; in number of opinions written he nearly always led the Court, and the pattern of his thinking became far more original. This was a period of excellent judicial output.

Having licked the problem of doing his job, Clark's third five years added a new element to his life and work. His tremendous efforts, earlier and continued, had made him a recognized national Bar and judicial leader and he undertook the duties of leadership. He took over the chairmanship of the Section of Judicial Administration of the American Bar Association and has turned it into an effective working unit. Its budget has risen from $3,000 to $50,000 during his period of leadership.

During this period, in 1961, the Kellogg Foundation allotted $345,000 to be expended by the Joint Committee of seventeen national organizations under his direction within a three-year period for training programs for state trial judges of every state. In each state the trial judges are polled to determine the most pressing problems of their jurisdiction. The staff of the project then reduces these to five key legal subjects, and prepares written materials showing the experience of the other states in dealing with those particular matters. A three-day session follows for all of the trial judges in the state, with these carefully prepared materials having been previously furnished to each of them. The judges meet in panels on each of the five problems with a law professor usually serving as reporter for each panel. At the conclusion a general assembly of all of the judges hears the five reporters on the principal conclusions reached.

Whenever possible, Clark personally attends these meetings. His attendance is by no means mere window dressing—he sits through extended discussions, listening patiently to what must often be tedious repetition to a person of his broad experience. He then tactfully but directly makes incisive suggestions as to how the problems of the particular state may be solved.

In this he is completely outspoken. For illustration, in 1959, the Justice spoke to the Arizona State Bar. In a gracious way he found everything on which the state could possibly be complimented, but the talk was by no means a shower of roses. He reminded his audience that the state had a woefully high crime rate and that its judges were seriously underpaid. He told the State Supreme Court that it could cut down on its ever enlarging backlog only by drastically shortening its opinions. He noticed that the trial courts were falling farther and farther behind in the state's principal city. He advised the Bench and the Bar not to procrastinate, and put forth specific suggestions for action. His argument was persuasive and many of his suggestions were adopted. Four years later, he came back to the state, reviewed the situation, and in a general address forthrightly told the State Supreme Court what he thought it had done right and what he thought it had done wrong by way of improvement. Clark is blessed with a capacity to make suggestions without giving offense, and his observations went down well. His success with the Kellogg Foundation project has been so great that, without solicitation, the President of the Foundation approached him concerning a new grant of $300,000 to be expended over a three-year period for a college for state trial judges which will be under Clark's general direction and is to be held annually at the University of Colorado for a month during the summer.

Cases are first decided by a vote of the Court and then assigned to a Justice for the writing of the opinion. In the beginning, Clark, as a novice on the Court, upon receiving an assignment had his law clerks draw up a draft memorandum on the case outlining the facts, authorities and suggested lines of thought while he, simultaneously, worked up a first draft of the opinion itself. From these drafts and subsequent discussions both with his law clerks and other Justices he would compose the ultimate opinion for the Court. This plan proved both cumbersome and time consuming, and he has since prepared all drafts of the opinions at his home, usually in longhand but more recently sometimes by dictating. After typing, he has referred them to his clerks for checking as to accuracy of facts, quotations, and citations. As for petitions for certiorari, his clerks go over them first, giving him memoranda on each which outline the facts, the issues, controlling cases if any, and whether there are disagreements among the lower Courts. Clark studies these along with the original papers in preparation for the Court's weekly conference at which he discusses the petitions with the other Justices and casts his vote. The Clark opinions reveal a most incisive, natural, and personal style.

On the Bench, Clark has probably written as many important antitrust decisions as any other Justice in American history. In these, as in his other cases, his style for the past many years has been vivid and vigorous, but almost invariably temperate. Perhaps the only opinion he has written on which he may have been overvigorous was his dissent on the *Jencks* case, mentioned above, involving the circumstances under which the prosecution is required to reveal its documents to the defense in criminal cases. He expressed the fear that under the majority opinion, "those intelligence agencies of our government engaged in law enforcement may as well close up shop for the Court has opened their files to the criminal and thus afforded him a Roman holiday for rummaging through confidential information as well as vital national secrets." While Clark in retrospect may think that his language was a little extreme, his basic conviction on the merits of his position remains unchanged.

While *Jencks* may overdo it, it nonetheless illustrates a talent for using simple phrases pungently. In a recent concurrence, he spoke of the Court's opinion as one which, as if "shearing a hog, comes up with little wool."

When he felt that the Court was demanding more of state procedure than it was demanding of itself, he said, "Indeed, if the Court is correct, it may be that we should first clean up our own house. . . . There is an old adage which my good Mother used to quote to me, i.e., 'People who live in glass houses had best not throw stones.' I dissent."

He has a concise way with him as when he summarized a matter in a sentence recently, saying, "The Court's decision today, then, does no more than raise a distinction which has no basis in logic and an increasingly eroded basis in authority."

Clark's three outstanding opinions of recent years have been very outstanding indeed. His leading search-and-seizure opinion extended the full protection of the federal constitutional provisions to all state law-enforcement practices. The topic was genuinely difficult and the opinion is a model of lucid persuasiveness. His prayer opinion, on the impropriety of requiring even the Lord's Prayer as a compulsory religious exercise in schools, while clearly in accord with previous Court decisions, is exceptionally well expressed. His individual opinion in the leading case requiring equal distribution of voters among election districts is, as a practical matter, probably the most important subject on which he has ever written; for the redistricting cases should change the entire political complexion of the United States by breaking the stranglehold of underpopulated districts over Congress and the state legislatures. The clarity of Clark's opinion has resulted in its being used, followed and quoted as much as the opinion of the Court, especially the phrase "crazy quilt" which he used to describe the pattern of invidious discrimination present in the Tennessee apportionment.

It was for this reason, and for his progression from the career service to the Court, that in 1960 the Federal Bar Association granted a "Justice Tom C. Clark award" for career lawyers in the District of Columbia. The National Lawyers Club displayed only two portraits, one of its founder and the other of Clark. The Club House Committee explains that it has hung the Clark picture at the entrance "so that all might see as they come in the man who best exemplifies the finest career in Government."

In 1962, the American Bar Association and the American Judicature Society gave Clark their highest award. The American Bar Gold Medal was for "Conspicuous Service to the Cause of American Jurisprudence." While the medal was well warranted, a more inappropriate title has rarely been selected. Clark is the very opposite of conspicuous. When, in 1962, his picture was portrayed about the country in a national billboard campaign for traffic safety, it was probably the first time the great bulk of Americans had seen him at all. The general personal impression is of a gray man. The gray of his hair and his easy quietness can make him extremely inconspicuous. His two most conspicuous personal traits are modesty and courtesy. He is totally incapable of bragging on himself (a phrase he uses); his intuitive instinct is to minimize his own accomplishments. As to any given achievement, his attitude is, "I didn't do anything, it was somebody else who got that done"; or "I just tried to give it a little hand where I could." This is not a pose or a casual impression; he is consistently a man who does not claim credit and prefers to give it to others. He is a person who does not think in "I" terms at all.

The Justice's wife, Mary Ramsey Clark, the daughter of a Texas Supreme Court Justice, and the "good soldier" of the moves from Texas to Washington to New Orleans to the West Coast and back again, is the vivacious member of the family. She is a constantly bubbling southern lady with a Texas accent, a remarkable talent for names, and a warmth of personality that makes her a favorite among Washington hostesses. The couple have two children, a married daughter and a son who for three years has served as an Assistant Attorney General in the Department of Justice, and six grandchildren.

The Justice rarely writes for publication, except in his Court work. One of the few exceptions was an article for a national magazine on the place of religion in America—he thinks it belongs in the home, and, as a good Presbyterian, in the church. In that essay, he spoke of the kind of men whom America needs as "Men who prefer honor to wealth, truth to sophistry, kindness to covetousness, modesty to vaingloriousness, service to recognition, humility to grandeur, usefulness to reward."

He had written a very good description of Mr. Justice Clark.

Chapter Six

MR. JUSTICE

John Marshall Harlan

WHAT'S in a name?" in one instance is eighty years on the Supreme Court of the United States. Today's Justice John Marshall Harlan is named for his grandfather, who served on the Court from 1877 to 1911. The former Justice John Marshall Harlan in turn was named for John Marshall (no family connection) who served on the Court from 1801 to 1835. No name is more closely connected with Supreme Court history than that of the present Justice.

The current Harlan inherits a strong streak of independence along with his name. His grandfather cut his own course on the Supreme Court and was more than once in lone dissent on matters on which time has later paid great respect to his judgments. The most famous instance was the grandfather's "Constitution is color blind" dissent in 1894 from the decision recognizing segregation. The present Justice's father, one of the great Theodore Roosevelt or Bull Moose Progressives, was the reform Mayor of Chicago, where Harlan was born in 1899.

Harlan's own legal career was spent largely on Wall Street, where he was a case-trying partner for one of the most famous firms in the country, the firm of which Thomas E. Dewey is now a senior partner. As a Wall Street lawyer, Harlan came to be representative of some of the great financial interests. At the same time he was an extraordinarily objective man. He had the capacity of all good lawyers of becoming the champion, heart and soul, of his client in any particular matter. But he restricted that enthusiasm to the particular case he was handling; the politics or prejudices of the client were the client's business, not Harlan's. Harlan developed the habit of an open mind.

That same quality has stuck with Harlan the judge, building into him that peculiar essence known as the judicial temperament. If some hypothetical prosecutor or District Attorney had to choose from among the nine members of the Supreme Court someone to try his case, he would probably not choose Harlan; he could probably find someone with more of a prosecutor's point of view. On the other hand, if, in the same case, a hypothetical defense lawyer had to pick a judge, he also would probably not pick Harlan; he could find someone on the Bench with more of a defense point of view. But if the prosecuting attorney and the defense attorney were required to agree on one of the nine to try that same case, then they very probably would choose Harlan whose even balance would give fairness to each.

Of the nine Justices, Harlan comes to the Court from the background of the greatest personal comfort. His mayor father could afford his excursion into politics. Harlan's elementary and preparatory schools, Chicago Latin, Appleby School, and Lake Placid School, tell the story of considerable ease. He did his college work at Princeton most successfully. On leaving Princeton, Harlan had the opportunity of going to England as a Rhodes Scholar. He consulted with H. Alexander Smith, later to be a United States Senator from New Jersey, feeling free to ask him for his advice on whether to accept the Rhodes Scholarship. Smith told him that anyone who had the opportunity to study the background of American law by studying English law in England certainly ought to take it. Harlan followed this advice, attending Oxford University from 1921 to 1923. His Oxford and English ties are still warmly meaningful to him and he prizes a continuing honorary attachment to his college.

While Harlan enjoys the comforts of life he tends to be a little deprecating about them. When he was appointed to the Court he had a seven-room apartment in New York City with a view of the river, and a nine-room house in Weston, Connecticut. He was a golfer, a fisherman, a Republican, and a Presbyterian. As he listed these off to an interviewer he said apologetically, "It does sound awfully tame and correct, doesn't it? If it helps any, we don't have a terribly *good* view of the river—sort of an on-an-angle one—and I don't play golf at all well. Professionally, there have been very few lurid moments, though I did prosecute Earl Carroll for perjury in connection with that matter of a lady bathing in champagne at one of his parties."

Harlan first hit the news and the road to fame when as a young man he was an assistant to Emory Buckner, senior partner of the firm with which he served so long but then United States Attorney in New York. He finished this work in 1927, but was called into New York State service in 1928 when Alfred E. Smith was Governor of New York and Jimmy Walker was mayor of the city. The Borough President for the Borough of Queens was involved in a sewer scandal, charged with having made money on the laying of sewers. Harlan, as an assistant to the investigating commission, presented evidence for it and later became prosecutor of those charged. He did a good job; it was his first taste of real distinction.

When Buckner came back to the firm from which he had taken Harlan in the first place, Harlan returned with him and settled down to the trial of civil cases. His chief, Buckner, had for many years been one of New York's great trial lawyers. Harlan in time succeeded to many of Buckner's duties and to much of his distinction.

The first really great case was the Wendel will contest. Ella Wendel died leaving an estate of some $40,000,000 to $50,000,000. She was, at best, an eccentric recluse, and the last of a rich line. The lawyer who had drawn her will was a beneficiary under it, and her capacity to make a will—more bluntly, her plain sanity at the time she signed it—was questionable. There was indeed a pile of gold, and everyone in New York in the early thirties who needed a nickel and who had a little ingenuity headed for it.

Ella Wendel's will left most of her fortune to five charities. Her executors, needing a trial attorney to protect the honey pot against the flies, chose Buckner as chief counsel, with Harlan as his assistant, and with Henry Friendly, now a federal appeals judge, as Harlan's assistant. Buckner shortly became ill, and there was a genuine question as to whether Harlan, by then only thirty-two years of age, was ready for the responsibility of protecting the estate; but the executors after due deliberation decided that Harlan was their man, and it became his case.

For reasons which have been suggested, the will was not hard to challenge; but the only legitimate challengers were relatives entitled to some portion of the estate for themselves. A horde of people rapidly claimed to be relatives of the late Ella. The five charities put genealogists to work, and the problem of the attorneys was to find out who really were the relatives and then settle as best they could.

After thorough research, it developed that there were nine relatives, some with the charities and some with the contestants. Meanwhile, a gentleman named Morris turned up claiming to be Ella's brother. Harlan went to Scotland, this being the ancestral home of the Wendels, to take depositions, leaving Friendly and a small staff to mop up on the claimants in the United States. It was typical of Harlan's thoroughness that he had established some twenty-three different tests to prove that some of those claiming to be relatives were frauds. Upon his return from Scotland, Friendly met with him and reported with some pride that it had been possible to establish for twenty-one different reasons that most of the claimants had no Wendel blood in their veins. Friendly was content; but when he received the report, Harlan, with his unlimited zeal for perfection, quietly asked that the other two grounds be nailed down also.

The eventual trial, in which Harlan was thoroughly successful, was typical of his tactics. In his dealings with opposing counsel, Harlan was always perfect courtesy; he wanted to defeat the other side but not to be unpleasant to it. He had the extraordinary accomplishment of being a victorious lawyer whose opponents liked him. This same quality is reflected in his many dissents on the Supreme Court today; they may be strong but they are never unpleasant.

Harlan's Number One victims were liars. Because of his utter thoroughness, he always knew his case inside out, down to the smallest detail. If some witness told a story conflicting with the known truth, Harlan led the witness on until he had told his story thoroughly and completely. Then, on further examination, he would develop the proof which made a conspicuous liar out of the witness. In the *Wendel* case not only were the fake claims knocked out, but the Court found one witness so untrustworthy that the trial judge directed the District Attorney to prosecute him for perjury.

Harlan is remembered by the lawyers who worked for him in the thirties as always pleasant and always demanding. His clerks have the same experience with him on the Supreme Court; they always feel comfortably free to go in to see him at any time. Harlan was a hard worker, much given to night labors, with a clear notion of where he was going and just what he wanted. He had relatively few jury cases; he was at his best in court matters.

Preparation and organization of cases, even where they covered thousands of documents, were Harlan's outstanding achievements; on the law points he was also well prepared. He was not lightning quick either in sizing up the case or in examining a witness, nor was he slower than average. He was simply very, very thorough. Anyone who learned under Buckner was likely to be careful with his facts, and so with Harlan.

Harlan was a courthouse lawyer, trying cases and preparing them for trial year in and year out. At times he was so busy he could not even read the newspapers. His cultural interests probably suffered a little. While well rounded, he did not give a dominant attention to art, or symphony or opera; it was law on which he focused all the time.

At the beginning of World War II, Harlan, then forty-two years of age, was a seasoned veteran of the New York Bar. He then left his firm to go into the service. A unit had been established to advise General Spaatz, the Commanding General of the Eighth Army Air Force. Harlan headed it, and his section had active responsibility for the bombing operations on the European Continent. He personally made repeated bombing expeditions, and on his recommendations, many changes in bombing methods were made. He came out of the war a Colonel, the recipient of the Legion of Merit from the United States and the Croix de Guerre from the French.

At the conclusion of the war, Harlan returned to his New York firm, continuing there until his appointment to the Court of Appeals in 1954. The only substantial interruption came in 1951 when for some eight months he was the Chief Counsel for Governor Dewey's New York State Crime Commission. Harlan had not known Dewey more than casually previously, but the Crime Commission was clearly serious business, and so Harlan accepted the duty.

During the practice portion of these postwar years, Harlan handled several antitrust cases. When the Government brought an action to force a separation between the General Motors Corporation and the Du Pont Company interests, Harlan was counsel for the senior members of the Du Pont family, Irénée and Pierre. In this capacity he guided the general strategy for the defense. He took many depositions, saw thousands of documents, and worked so hard that many of his friends became worried for his health. Harlan was physically always a fragile man and has occasionally had some serious illnesses. His most difficult task was to help his elderly witnesses dredge up from their memories events of the years 1913 to 1917, which were critical to the case. His tactics were always workmanlike, not dramatic; he was well mannered and quiet spoken, his temper occasionally flaring in anger but never in rudeness.

As Harlan's personal distinction increased, he received the invitations which commonly come to the prominent to engage in extra-curricular activities. In 1952, Justice Owen J. Roberts of the Supreme Court invited Harlan to join the Atlantic Union Committee, an organization, described by Roberts to Harlan, as one intended to help the states bordering the Atlantic Ocean to grow into some sort of a group with common authority which would give the United States the power to enforce peace. The Union was a high prestige activity, its program sponsored in 1951 by twenty-eight United States Senators. Harlan was pleased with the invitation but was aware that as a trial lawyer he could not give the program any serious attention. He therefore accepted with the understanding that he would be inactive. He attended no meetings and paid no dues. His name, however, was on the letterhead, though without his actual knowledge.

Since much of Harlan's work was in the antitrust field, the leading Government antitrust lawyers came to know him. An experienced Government opponent thought him one of the ablest representatives of industry in the United States, a man of balance and integrity. Another, the head of the Antitrust Division, also thought him an effective and honorable opponent.

In February of 1954, President Eisenhower appointed Harlan to the Court of Appeals for the Second Circuit, the area which covers New York, Connecticut, and Vermont. He was advanced by President Eisenhower to the Supreme Court on November 9, 1954, in place of Robert H. Jackson, and since his nomination could not be acted on at that Session of the Congress, he was re-appointed by the President at the next term.

The hearing on Harlan's appointment before the Senate Judiciary Committee is a colorful illustration of grass-roots democracy when it is being just a little eccentric. In sheer volume, one Senator reported he received more opposition mail than he had received on any similar matter. The charges were essentially these:

1. Some persons felt that it was unpatriotic of Harlan to have studied in England at all and that he should never have accepted a Rhodes Scholarship. Senator Smith of New Jersey turned up to take full responsibility for that decision on the part of the nominee.

2. A charge was made that Harlan was the grandson of the previous Justice Harlan, and that his grandfather had dissented from the opinion upholding the validity of segregation. Harlan came on for confirmation only a few months after the Supreme Court had held that

Grandfather Harlan had been right in the first place. A lady representing an organization called the Wheel of Progress read excerpts from various publications to the Committee to the effect that "Ike couldn't have done much better even if he had appointed a Negro member."

3. The most voluble opposition was directed at Harlan because of his membership in the Atlantic Union. A representative of the Maryland State Society of the Order of the American Revolution objected on this ground, and on the additional ground that Harlan had been a Rhodes Scholar, which the ladies thought a most unhappy circumstance.

While several members of the Senate Judiciary Committee seemed inclined to agree with the Daughters of the Revolution that the Atlantic Union was an undesirable project, Senator Kefauver of the same Committee happened to be a strong supporter of it. Since the Chairman of the Judiciary Committee had been one of its Senate sponsors, the Union was hard to attack. However, an organization called the American Coalition of New York, which covered some one hundred subsidiary organizations, among them the Colonial Order of the Acorn (the New York Chapter), the Westchester Security League, and two dozen organizations variously Sons or Daughters of the Revolution or of Liberty, felt that there was "no excuse for taking any chances with" anyone who was in favor of world government.

Harlan was in the unhappy position that he really had only the most casual understanding of the Atlantic Union, having done nothing but send an amiable note of acquiescence to Justice Roberts; and yet he did not wish to wash his hands of a cause in which, if he had participated, he would probably have warmly approved. Having made a gesture toward the Atlantic Union without really understanding it, he did not wish to appear to abandon it. As he said, from whatever he did know about the principles of the Atlantic Union organization, it was thoroughly commendable. When asked questions about the Bricker Amendment, a proposal to amend the Constitution to cut down the treaty power, Harlan acknowledged that as a trial lawyer moving from case to case he really had only the vaguest idea of what the Bricker Amendment was.

4. The Judiciary Committee of this moment happened to have on it an exceptionally large number of Republicans who were unenthusiastic about their own party's former Presidential candidate, Thomas E. Dewey. Dewey had gone into Harlan's own firm shortly after Harlan had left it, and this suggested a degree of identity between Harlan and Dewey which annoyed the anti-Deweyites. Harlan's testimony was that Dewey came to the firm after he had left it to go on the Court of Appeals, and that the matter had not been considered prior to his appointment. Again, he in no way diminished the stature of Governor Dewey; it simply happened that as a matter of fact, his own appointment to the Court and Dewey's to the firm had been unconnected events.

5. Finally, someone appeared to complain that Harlan, when Chief Counsel for the Crime Commission, had given him a hard time. The Committee considered his lament with greater patience than posterity is likely to show, and it will perhaps suffice to say that he had no legitimate grounds for objection. After 182 pages of hearings had accumulated, Harlan was easily confirmed.

The qualities which a man looks for in another are likely to be those which he cherishes in himself. In 1962, Justice Charles E. Whittaker retired from the Court. Harlan was called upon to say a word on this occasion, a task pleasantly accepted because he esteemed Whittaker affectionately. His description was this:

Justice Whittaker was a prodigious worker who was satisfied with nothing less than full mastery of every record and brief. When circumstances made it impossible to realize that goal, he regarded it as a matter for self-reproach. While a man of intense convictions he was always open minded, and in close cases one could never feel that he was beyond persuasion until the last word had been spoken or written on the issues. He had an innate sense of fairness but always strove against yielding up a sound legal conclusion to the compassionate circumstances of a particular case or to his personal ideologies-temptations which make the art of judging the more exacting, and sometimes interrupt the evenhanded application of the law.

Whether this is or is not an accurate description of Justice Whittaker is, for this purpose, an irrelevant matter. But certainly, it would be impossible to find a better description of Mr. Justice Harlan. He is disembodied, impersonal justice. He is also a man at peace with himself; he has complete confidence that, so much as a human can achieve it, he will declare the law objectively. He knows that his instincts may carry him in one direction or another, but he tries hard not to be dominated by them.

As a civilized human being, Harlan frequently has clear notions of what the law ought to be but he does not regard himself as employed by the people of the United States for the purpose of making it. Particularly in interpreting Acts of Congress, he is absolutely content if he thinks he knows what Congress meant; indeed, he may occasionally have a false serenity, finding purposes which others do not see. The result of an interpretation may make good sense or no sense, but this is the problem of Congress; as he is fond of saying, it is "for Congress, not the courts, to change the statute. We must deal with the statute as we find it."

The Harlan peace of mind is particularly evident in the applications which come to him as an individual Justice. The country is divided into regions, each made the primary responsibility of some one Justice. Where some order is needed which must be entered before there is time for the Court to consider it, the regional Justice must consider whether the order shall be entered. For example, if someone is sentenced to death by a state court, and wishes to appeal to the United States Supreme Court, the matter may come up in the summertime when the Court is not in session. If someone should be sentenced in July for execution in August, it will be of very little interest to him what the Supreme Court might decide if only he were around to hear it in October.

A typical example of such a summertime appeal is the matter of a person named Edwards, convicted of murder and sentenced to death by the State of New York. Harlan had to decide not whether Edwards should win his case, but rather whether, in Harlan's opinion, the other Justices would, if they were available, think it should be held for decision. He had to make an intelligent guess as to what his fellow members of the Court would think was the law if they were asked. The lawyers who had brought the case to him felt strongly about it, and Harlan went out of his way to say that the lawyers "have done their utmost for petitioner, but nothing has been shown which would justify me in interfering with this stern course of the state's judgment." He concluded, "Realizing the heavy responsibility which rests on a single Justice of this Court where life is at stake, I can only conclude that there is no substance to petitioner's effort to obtain a further review of his conviction by this Court, and that it is my duty to deny this application."

Harlan is a judge who calls them as he sees them without any particular philosophic preconception except that he should apply the law in the particular case as he understands it. In the *Edwards* case, just described, he saw no merit in the application—and, indeed, there does not appear to be any—and so he let the man be executed. But he is not unsympathetic to the plight of those charged with crime. On the contrary, he wishes to see that they get precisely the protection which the Constitution affords them. For example, on the matter of self-incrimination and the plea of the Fifth Amendment, he has regularly taken the position that "an unfavorable inference should not be drawn from the mere fact that the Fifth Amendment privilege has been invoked."

Harlan's long trial experience gives him complete understanding of the practicalities of trials, and he would put up with no improprieties. An illustration is a case tried in Bucks County, Pennsylvania, in which a number of defendants were charged with murder in the course of a robbery. The defendants were almost certainly guilty of both, but there was doubt as to whether the proper sentence should be life imprisonment or death. The defendants were not tried together, and as it happened the first to be tried came on before a respected local judge, who gave very strong public statements indicating his own sense of outrage at the defendants. When the second case was tried, the judge in the first case, though not trying the matter, spent considerable time in the courtroom, and took a very active interest in the prosecution. Harlan thought this improper, and believed a new trial was required. He felt that the first judge's "manifest interest in the trial," particularly in a community where he could be expected to be well known to the jury, amounted to support for the prosecution and might "have tipped the scales for the jury in favor of a death verdict."

Harlan regularly carries protection of civil liberties less far than would, for example, Chief Justice Warren or Justices Black, Douglas, and others. However, he has also written some of the leading civil liberties opinions of recent years. In the *Federal Loyalty Program* case, the issue was the power of a Government agency to dismiss without trial a food and drug inspector charged with having had "sympathetic association" with certain suspicious organizations or a "close association" with persons regarded as undesirable. This is the so-called "guilt by association"—that is to say, the charge is not that the individual did anything in particular but that he associated with other people who either had or were likely to do something.

Harlan held that if any person was to be dismissed without a hearing for any such hazy offense as improper associations, he must certainly be someone in a security position of some consequence. He held that, under the law, the President had no power to authorize such dismissals throughout the federal service. As he saw it, "It is difficult to justify summary suspensions and unreviewable dismissals on loyalty grounds of employees who are not in 'sensitive' positions and who are thus not situated where they could bring about any discernible adverse effects on the nation's security. In view of the stigma attached to persons dismissed on loyalty grounds, the need for procedural safeguards seems even greater than in other cases, and we will not lightly assume that Congress intended to take away those safeguards in the absence of some overriding necessity, such as exists in the case of employees handling defense secrets."

Harlan's most famous opinion in the civil liberties field is the so-called "Second String Communist" case, in which fourteen Communists were indicted in California on a double-barreled charge. The first was that they had *organized* a party to overthrow the Government of the United States; the second was that they had *advocated* or *encouraged* its overthrow through their activities. Harlan's opinion required an acquittal of several of the defendants and a new trial as to the rest.

On the organizational part of the case, Harlan found that the charge came too late. The Communist Party was organized for the first time in 1919. It was organized for a second time in 1945. Under the federal law, an action must be filed within three years of the event, and the indictments were filed in 1951, more than three years after either event.

This was a comparatively unimportant technical detail. The serious branch of the case was in the definition of the kind of advocacy which, within the limits of the rights of all Americans to free speech, can be punished under the Constitution.

Harlan's opinion held that advocacy of the overthrow of the Government can be punished when it instigates action to overthrow the Government. It may not be punished when it involves only promotion of abstract principle. The problem raised a fundamental issue in American democracy. The general meaning of freedom of speech is that all persons may advocate whatever they please. Americans rely on the truth, not the penitentiary, to conquer error. But no one has a freedom to advocate immediate, direct, concrete action to overthrow the Government. Harlan held that the Smith Act was directed at action, not at advocacy, and that some incitement to direct illegal action had to be proved to convict under that law. Applying this standard, Harlan found the evidence as to five of the defendants too thin to permit retrial. The other nine could be retried on a proper standard.

Harlan can comfortably make tight distinctions. In another Communist prosecution he wrote the five-to-four opinion upholding their conviction. Harlan held that active membership in the organization, where the organization was engaged in illegal advocacy of reasonably immediate action, was enough to warrant a conviction. The instructions to the jury were to determine whether the Communist defendants were encouraging persons to stand ready, as speedily as circumstances permit, to overthrow the Government. If the jury found this, he believed that a person was properly convicted under the law and the Constitution.

Harlan's opinions are of two distinct types. Some are most comprehensive; each of the cases just mentioned are very thorough. His 1964 opinion on Cuba's taking of sugar properties is a prodigy of thoroughness. Others, particularly in dissent, consist of brief statements. Harlan's work method is that sometimes he writes a first draft and sometimes he has his clerks do so. If he does the first draft, it is likely to be fairly well perfected by the time he is done with it; he puts in the citations, examines the record to check the details, looks up his cases, and generally does the whole job. The work his clerks give him, he revises to his own satisfaction. Sometimes the opinion is mixed, with a division of subject matters so that his aides do preliminary work on one section while he does another.

Because of Harlan's easy manner with any staff assistants, the simplest way to take up problems is orally. After he has prepared a draft, he invites criticism from the clerks and after study, they make their criticisms. Early in a term, when the office is less busy, his clerks may also be able to prepare memoranda on the cases for him before the lawyers present them orally. Later, as the work intensifies, this is likely to be replaced by general discussion of the more interesting cases before they are heard.

Harlan learned to work hard forty years ago and he has the habit. He puts in a full day at the Court and takes work home at day's end. For him, some matters don't take much research. On a question of whether a trial court properly took a matter away from a jury, he thinks the issue should never come to the Supreme Court at all; and so these cases do not take much time. For an opposite illustration, in difficult trade-mark cases, he takes all the time he needs.

In 1962 Justice Frankfurter resigned from the Court and was replaced by Justice Goldberg. Frankfurter had been Harlan's closest intellectual ally on the Court. The shift in personnel has tended to leave him rather alone, forcing up the number of his dissenting opinions in marked degree. At the 1961 term of the Court, Harlan had fourteen dissenting opinions and twenty-two the next year; he had thirty-four dissenting votes in 1961 and forty-six in 1962, a figure almost 50 per cent higher than the next Justice. In 1963–1964 the number of his individual dissents continued high. There is no particular philosophical line which, without forcing of the matter, distinguishes his position from that of his fellow Justices; he is simply an everlastingly independent soul and he conducts himself that way.

But while the lonely can quickly become the acid pen, Harlan's never does. With this heavier load of self-expression to carry he is frequently very brief, but he is always clear, cogent, direct, and appealing. Harlan in dissent is still Harlan, a temperate and considerate man. As an old friend has said of him, "He's such a *decent* fellow—he never forgets you." Harlan does not forget, and he feels strongly, as he has said, that "ill-informed or intemperate criticism of the doings of the courts only serves to breed misunderstanding and ultimately disrespect for the law." He will not contribute to that disrespect, no matter what his differences.

John Harlan stands high with his colleagues. He deserves to. He has character beyond reproach, workmanship hard to equal, and a gift for turning a good sentence. Any good Court is a composite of many talents. Harlan has observed that not "all deficiencies in our society which have failed of correction by other means should find a cure in the courts," a view which needs expression. The law is a field of close distinctions and fine gradations, of cases which because they are a little bit different one from another require different results. Whether he agrees with his fellow Justices or not, Harlan achieves better performance for them all by his insistent probing for a true base of decision.

Chapter Seven

MR. JUSTICE
William Brennan

A GREAT AMERICAN historian once declared that all the figures of American history could be classified by one simple test: Which would and which would not make good next-door neighbors? The test is surprisingly easy to apply. It is really very unlikely that anyone ever wandered over to Mount Vernon or to Hyde Park to ask George Washington or Franklin D. Roosevelt for the use of a lawn mower. On the other hand the neighbors probably stood in line of a Saturday afternoon to see whether Abraham Lincoln or Harry Truman was using his gardening equipment.

Applying this test, Bill Brennan clearly is the world's most natural next-door neighbor. There have in the past been some dreadful curmudgeons on the Supreme Court. Examples are the men of frozen deportment, as they were likely to be called in the early nineteenth century; the old hippopotamus, as Mr. Justice Miller was less than fondly described in the late nineteenth century; the old [unprintable] as Justice McReynolds was regarded in the twentieth century. The current Court has none such—each of the Justices has very human qualities. But if the members of the Court were to borrow from the Miss America contest and elect a Mr. Congeniality, Brennan would win hands down.

With this personal quality, Brennan combines great diligence, great effectiveness, and great modesty. When Brennan was appointed in 1956, Max Freedman in the *Manchester Guardian* began his report, " 'With great merit and even greater modesty,' says Montaigne, 'one can remain unknown for a long time.' " Brennan continues to remain both inconspicuous and effective. His influence on the Court has been extraordinary. Few new Justices have written as many genuinely important opinions for the Court as Justice Brennan in his first seven years.

One of Brennan's rare tart moments, which resulted in a nationwide news story, came in the summer of 1963 when he spoke on public criticism of the Court. "The Court does not and should not escape criticism," he said. "People don't have to agree with the decisions if they are successfully able to refute them." However, he thought the newspaper attacks on the school-prayer opinions an example of premature criticism. The opinions covered some one hundred and nine pages, he said, and, "Yet within two hours the critics were in print saying the Court was wrong." He thought that the critics should at least read the decisions first. As he said: "These opinions are the product of literally months of studying, reading, writing, revision, checking and then more of the same again. Yet within two or three hours after the opinions were read in open court, distinguished public figures all over the country were bluntly passing judgment on the Court's action on radio, television, and in the newspapers. Proper analysis of these opinions would have taken much longer."

For another illustration of his directness, in an essay on criminal law Brennan expressed his concern that not enough talented lawyers were going into criminal defense. He put the responsibility squarely on the law schools, saying: "I think the law schools have to share some of the blame for this lack of what should be widespread devotion to the tradition. If the law schools give only cursory attention to criminal procedure in the curriculum, it is hard to see how students can be blamed for coming away from law school with the feeling that perhaps the institution also shares the unfortunate tendency of the community to disapprove of lawyers who undertake the defense of people charged with crime."

These statements are typical of Brennan's forthrightness. For all of his easy amiability, his extraordinary directness is the most remarkable quality of his personal conversation. When he speaks informally, he drops into a highly colloquial English, speaking with the utmost candor, with evident sincerity, and completely without guile.

When Brennan was appointed to the Court, *Time* magazine described him as "the happy Irishman." On the Irish side of that definition he certainly qualifies. His father was in fact the Irish politician which Brennan looks like but is not. The father came from Ireland in 1880 and took his first job as a coal shoveler in a brewery. Later the father became a member of the Stationary Firemen's Union but, as Brennan's mother later recalled, the father "didn't like the way the union was run. Its office was in a saloon, the dues were paid to the saloonkeeper, and there was no accounting of the money. The saloonkeeper gave out the jobs." In due course Brennan's father campaigned to reform the union and became its business agent. In his administration, the books were available for inspection. When somebody gave him a box of tobacco, he had the givers come back and pick it up. In 1916 the father was serving as business agent of the International Brotherhood of Engineers and Oilers. The Mayor of Newark, a Republican, needed a Democrat for his police board, and appointed Brennan, Senior. Thereafter the father served as director of public safety or a police commissioner on an elective basis.

Justice Brennan was born in Newark on April 25, 1906. As the hour of delivery drew near, Dr. Haggerty of New Brunswick was sent for. A friend of the doctor was being married in St. Joseph's Church, and Haggerty arrived in striped pants and a morning coat, an outfit Brennan continues to see from time to time in arguments before the Court.

Unlike Justice Goldberg, who worked as a youngster from extreme necessity, Justice Brennan worked also but for his extras rather than for his actual existence. He delivered milk house-to-house in Newark and handed out change on trolley cars. His brother milked cows for the dairy for which Brennan delivered. He also worked as a filling-station attendant and as a delivery boy for a butcher and for a grocery store.

In high school he washed cars and changed tires in a garage and in college he earned his meals by being secretary of his college fraternity and did tutoring to buy his clothes.

For his higher education, Brennan went first to the University of Pennsylvania. The Boston Police Commissioner recommended Harvard Law School to his father as a place far enough away from the New York night spots so that a boy would stay busy. He was graduated from there near the top of his class in 1931.

Brennan practiced with a Newark firm, two of whose senior partners were the sons of a former Supreme Court Justice. One of his early tasks was to prepare a complete report on a certain point of law for one of the senior partners. Brennan worked day and night, weekdays and weekends, for three weeks, and then handed in a report over three hundred pages long. It was, beyond doubt, complete. This quality of completeness has been a staple of Brennan's work ever since, having about it something of blessing and something of curse. He follows the unusual practice of regularly having his clerks prepare bench memos or written summaries of the briefs, the authorities, the difficult questions, and everything there is to know about them. Sometimes these memos are relatively brief, thirty or forty pages. Sometimes, on serious matters, they may run three to four hundred pages.

As a result, when Brennan goes on the bench, he is thoroughly prepared, and the courtroom observers who have noticed his capacity to bring out the hard points in a case during argument are seeing the result of careful preliminary work. The only bad feature of his extraordinary preparation is that Brennan may on occasion find himself writing an opinion with more material than he either needs or can bring himself to throw away, and the result is that his opinions are sometimes longer than strictly necessary. He is aware of this problem and tries to condense, although this is a battle with his own habit of completeness which he rather frequently loses.

As son of a union business agent, Brennan had a keen interest in labor relations. As a lawyer he went into that field—on the employers' side. One of his earliest disputes, a matter in which his own role was minor, concerned labor relations in building the Pulaski Skyway across the New Jersey landscape toward the Hudson River and New York. Either before or after the war he represented Western Electric, Jersey Bell Telephone, Phelps Dodge, Celanese Corporation, American Hair and Felt, and the Associated General Contractors of New Jersey in labor matters. He also had other work. When he was not yet well known in Newark he was sent down to the police headquarters to look into a knifing. While there he was confused with an escaped prisoner and had to establish his own identity to get out. On the non-labor side of his practice, he tried the Doris Duke tax case and later participated in briefing it in the United States Supreme Court. The matter involved an assessment of some $238,000,000.

Politically, both before and after the war, Brennan was a Democrat but not an active one. He never held or sought any elective office. He was first, foremost, and all the time a hard-working lawyer. Associates in the postwar period, when his practice grew immense, recall him as working sometimes as much as fourteen to sixteen hours a day for six or seven days a week. He has always been an early riser, enjoying cooking the family breakfast and bringing the bacon to the precise shade of crispness anyone at the table may desire. All too often he reached his office at 8:00 A.M., and did not get home until 2:00 the next morning.

During the war Brennan volunteered and was given labor relations responsibilities principally in Washington, but for a year on the West Coast. As his service began, he went on leave rather than resign from his firm so that his income could continue. However, he quickly found himself dealing with labor matters which concerned companies which were also clients of the firm. He therefore resigned from the firm entirely, giving up his income so that he could carry on with his assigned duties. His initial work was in Ordnance, where large munitions plants, Government-built but operated by private industry, raised serious legal problems, particularly of labor relations. From this post he progressed to a dual assignment as Chief of the Labor Branch, Army Service Forces, and Assistant to Undersecretary Patterson, with duties also for the Air Force.

Another large part of his assignment was the recruitment of sufficient manpower to bring defense plants to the fullest point of production. Since America never had conscription for the factories, the task of getting enough men to work was a heavy one. He recalls, for example, that at the time of the first American bombing of the interior of Germany, American bomber planes could make the long flight but the fighter planes could not. As a result, great numbers of the unprotected bombers were shot down. It was necessary to increase production in many ways, as, for example, by putting special added fuel tanks on some fighter equipment. Brennan headed Patterson's team on the West Coast for the general solution of these problems of labor relations and of increased recruitment.

One of Brennan's projects was what he describes as a straight Madison Avenue gimmick. At a time when the Battle of Tarawa was then recent, Brennan had a major hand, along with many others in the service and in the entertainment industry, in having the whole battle re-enacted at the Hollywood Coliseum, with troops, planes, and at least the appearance of live fire. It was a first-class show, focused on making the West Coast realize what war production was doing. One hundred thousand people attended each of the three performances. These and other devices did improve the factory recruitment situation and did help boost output. Brennan left the Army as a Colonel with the Legion of Merit.

After the war, he came back to his law firm, which was renamed to include him. For three years he continued his intense pace, hitting a splendid income. During this period New Jersey began its court reform program under its great Chief Justice Alfred Vanderbilt. In a country which has states enough with court systems which fail sadly to serve the needs of their people, New Jersey had one of the worst, and one of the most complicated, and one of the most inefficient.

Brennan was one of those who campaigned to give legal authority to build a better system and, over the years, Vanderbilt achieved vast reforms.

In 1949, New Jersey's Republican Governor Driscoll asked Brennan to serve as a trial judge. Acceptance meant slashing his income, and he was not a rich man; but Brennan accepted for two reasons. First, he had been working far too hard. He was facing a physical breakdown from his extreme office labors; second, he had backed the reform movement, and when an appeal was made to him on the grounds of "put up or shut up," the appeal was hard to refuse. For a time he was able to get along on savings, and after these were gone the family lived on his salary. Neither luxury nor show have any appeal at all for Brennan, and he has been quite content.

In 1950, Brennan moved from the trial to the appellate section of the New Jersey trial court, and in 1952, he was appointed to the Supreme Court of New Jersey. On that Court he worked directly and closely with Vanderbilt, developing a very keen interest in judicial administration. There he pitched in with Vanderbilt to reform the practice. Vanderbilt gave him full credit for the successive editions of the *New Jersey Manual of Pretrial Practice,* instructions and procedures for moving cases more swiftly before they are called for trial.

Brennan was troubled, as conscientious judges always are, when different judges gave different sentences for what was substantially the same offense, recognizing the unfairness of having years of a man's life depend on which judge happened to sentence him. To improve the judges' own understanding of how the prisons were administered and what they were trying to do, Brennan conceived the idea of taking them through the state's institutions each year. His own interest in prisons was always keen. He thought they should not be used as human warehouses, where the convicted are dumped and forgotten. While he believed that many criminals are vicious and cannot be redeemed, many others seemed to him either physically or mentally handicapped. He felt that those who might be simply confused or frustrated by life should while in prison be given redirection, training, and guidance.

Brennan has felt that his own best work on the state Supreme Court was in the fields of state and county taxation. However, he was inevitably called upon to express himself in many other very human matters. In a dissent in a case in which the state declined to show the defendant a copy of his own confession, Brennan said, "It shocks my sense of justice that in these circumstances counsel for an accused facing a possible death sentence should be denied inspection of his confession." Where an attempt was made to bar a burlesque house in Newark, he expressed his fear that censorship would interfere with normal freedoms and substitute the personal morality of the judges. In his last opinion for the New Jersey Supreme Court, Brennan disbarred a New Jersey lawyer. His concern, he said, was not with scoundrels personally violating laws. He felt that the public would understand that any profession is bound to have a few men of poor character. Rather he was concerned with those lawyers whose conduct was not criminal but rather within the twilight zone of morality. "We discipline," he said, "not to punish but to purify the Bar, to increase its reputation and to protect the public and the Courts from fraud and imposition."

Brennan's period of service on the Courts of New Jersey came at approximately the same time as Senator Joseph McCarthy's prominence in the United States Senate. The Irish-Catholic judge in New Jersey was outspokenly critical of the Irish-Catholic Senator in Washington. In 1954, speaking to the Charitable Irish Society of Boston, Brennan spoke of "some current practices" which "seem reminiscent of the Salem witch hunts." Later in 1954, he said, with very direct reference to certain Congressional hearings, "Abuse of individual rights today takes on modern dress—not the rack and the screw, but the distorted press release with the distorted version of what happens at secret sessions; the slanted epithet at the hapless and helpless victim. There are hopeful signs that we, as a civilized and decent people, have in the nick of time become ashamed of our toleration of the barbarism that has marked proceedings at some hearings."

As the McCarthy balloon began to deflate in 1956, Brennan was again outspoken. He found reason for "pure joy and relief that our collective conscience has sickened of excesses and is demanding adoption of permanent and lasting reforms to curb abuses of investigative powers."

In the fall of 1956, shortly before the national election of that year, Justice Sherman Minton retired from the Supreme Court. In the May preceding, there had been a conference on judicial administration in Washington, in which Attorney General Herbert Brownell took a deep interest. Chief Justice Vanderbilt had planned to appear for New Jersey, but Vanderbilt became ill and sent Brennan. Brennan did participate actively, and a friendly and respectful personal relationship with Brownell began at that time. When the Minton vacancy came, it was good politics for President Eisenhower to appoint a Democrat and a Catholic; indeed there is a tale, though undocumented, that the President had promised Cardinal Spellman of New York that the next appointee would be a Catholic. There had been no one of that faith on the Court since 1949. Deputy Attorney General William Rogers, after the appointment, noted that at the time of the May meeting, Brownell and he had lunched with Brennan and had been particularly impressed by his understanding of the problems of courts getting ever farther behind in their work. Rogers added, "We were glad that he was both a Democrat and a Catholic."

But there were other Democrats and other Catholics who might have been chosen. The special plus in Brennan's favor was Chief Justice Vanderbilt. Vanderbilt had been actively associated with the political organization of New York's Governor Thomas E. Dewey, and Vanderbilt had himself aspired to the Chief Justiceship when President Eisenhower had appointed Warren. Vanderbilt did not wish to be an Associate Justice, but he did back Brennan; and it was something of a concession to him that Brennan was chosen. In addition, Eisenhower's Secretary of Labor James Mitchell and his special counsel, Bernard Shanley, were each Brennan fans and admirers. Each was doubtless asked about the appointment and endorsed Brennan, although these gestures of good will were probably less important than the three key qualities of Brennan's Catholicism, his friendship with Vanderbilt, and Brownell's regard. The final plus was that President Eisenhower preferred to appoint men already judges to the Supreme Court, and this took many of Brennan's possible competitors out of the field.

In September, Brennan received a call from Brownell saying in substance, "Come down for breakfast with me and then we'll go over to see the President." The President proposed the appointment and James B. Haggerty, the President's press secretary, reports that, "I never saw a man say yes so fast when the President asked him if he would take a job."

The Brennan family, in all its Irish magnitude, was unabashedly, uninhibitedly delighted. So were Brennan's friends. White House adviser Shanley was rendered almost incoherent with enthusiasm as he bubbled about Brennan's "tremendous personality" and spoke of his pleasure at the appointment of a man so "genuine from top to toe." *The New York Times* summarized the favorable response by beginning its report with a quote from an old friend, "Bill Brennan is a hell of a nice guy." Most of the stories reported his plain, personal warmth, as, for example, the Des Moines *Sunday Register* which said, "The five-foot-nine-inch New Jersey man gives the appearance of being a jolly, slightly portly Irishman with a happy-go-lucky approach that would be more suited to winning votes in ward politics than to judicial contemplation. Nothing could be more deceiving than the immediate first impression when Judge Brennan turns on that infectious smile and extends a warm hand or merely beams for the camera." The Justice, continued the report, can turn it on and turn it off, and when he turns to judging he is a man dedicated to the law and legal processes.

While the response was generally either favorable or completely uninformed—for Brennan was essentially unknown outside his own state—at least one person who did not think he was a "hell of a nice guy" was Senator McCarthy. The Senator quickly announced that he would oppose the confirmation, saying that while Brennan "makes fine speeches against Communism, he has been waging a guerrilla war against committees that pick up individual Communists by the scruff of the neck and expose them."

When Brennan was appointed, the Congress was not in session. The President could make a recess appointment, and Brennan could serve pending the Senate's vote on his confirmation at the next session of Congress. When the confirmation hearings came on in February of 1957, therefore, Brennan had already been a Justice for several months. He was strongly endorsed by both the Republican Senators from his state, H. Alexander Smith and Clifford Case. However, McCarthy declared that Brennan's opinions were "likely to harm our efforts to fight Communism." In view of the Republican endorsements from New Jersey, McCarthy could only sadly observe that, "I fear left-wing Democrats and 'modern Republicans' will roll over and play dead."

By this time, McCarthy had completely used up his credit with his fellow Senators. One of the McCarthy stunts had been to refer in his speeches, vaguely and indefinitely, to "documents," a word which sounded ominously official and which was likely to mean nothing. At the hearing of the Senate Judiciary Committee on Brennan, Senator Joseph O'Mahoney of Wyoming participated. McCarthy began by declaring that he had documents. O'Mahoney asked him to identify them. McCarthy replied that the documents were Brennan's speeches. "Your say so doesn't make them so," said O'Mahoney. "I just want you to proceed in an orderly manner." When it came McCarthy's turn to examine Brennan, the Justice refused to answer many of his questions on the ground that they involved matters on which he would have to pass as a judge. On March 19, 1957, Brennan was confirmed, with McCarthy casting the only dissenting vote.

Brennan had been on the bench only briefly when he began to make his presence decisively felt. The first significant act was on a rehearing in a matter which had been decided the previous June by a sharply divided Court. The resignation of Justice Minton, before the rehearing could be passed upon, left the Court without a stated majority for any result and the Court, granting the rehearing before Brennan took his seat, largely put the matter up to Brennan to decide. At issue was the right of American citizens, usually wives abroad with the troops in foreign countries, to the usual constitutional rights of American citizens if they should be charged with crimes while they were abroad. The Court first held that the wives could be tried by military courts without such rights as trial by jury. Brennan joined the first dissenters and reversed the result.

The big case for Brennan's first year was *Jencks*. In this case, the defendant was charged with an offense which depended on events which had occurred some years before. The Government offered testimony of two persons who had been paid by the F.B.I. to gather information, each of whom testified as to statements the defendant was supposed to have made to them some years before. The defense contended that these statements were never made.

The issue was whether the defense was entitled, for purposes of cross-examination, to see the reports these F.B.I. employees had made at the time of the alleged statements, to see whether they had ever reported anything of the sort then, when the matter was current.

Justice Brennan for the Court held that the defense was entitled to see the reports the men made at the time. "Justice requires no less," said Brennan, "than that the defense should be allowed to decide whether the on-the-spot reports differed from what the witnesses many years later said from the stand."

The conclusion would seem self-evident, particularly because one of the very same witnesses turned out to be so untruthful that in another case the Government itself had to disavow his testimony. However, Congress for a time became vastly alarmed that F.B.I. reports would be inadequately protected. After some turmoil, it passed what is known as the Jencks Act, which appears largely to confirm Brennan's opinion.

The Chief Justice assigns the writing of opinions, and by tradition, the new Justices are likely to get a larger proportion than their seniors of the uninteresting cases. However, for a variety of reasons, Brennan very swiftly was writing on major matters. The biggest and most important matter on which he has ever written—indeed, the most important matter, aside from the basic segregation cases to come before the Court during Warren's Chief Justiceship—was the leading reapportionment case.

The reapportionment case arose from Tennessee. That state had not redistricted since 1901. Meanwhile, population had greatly shifted, so that, for example, Moore County, with 2,300 people, had as many representatives in the Tennessee State Legislature as Rutherford County with 25,000. This meant that a voter in Moore County had more than ten times the voting power of a citizen of Rutherford.

Such a situation strikes at the vitals of a democratic system which assumes that the voters are equal. If ten voters have the same weight as one hundred, then the voters are not equal at all. And there are equivalents of the Moore-Rutherford situation all over America.

The Brennan opinion held that if the legislature will not straighten out these situations, the courts may do so. This situation exists wherever legislatures fail to keep the district in step with the population shifts. This condition existed in England more than two hundred years ago, where some districts finally had no population but a few sheep. Such districts were called "pocket boroughs" because the lord of the manor could simply appoint someone to go to Parliament. Such a pocket-borough system has been developing in the United States since about 1900, and has existed in some states even longer. The Brennan opinion means that this must stop; there are not to be pocket boroughs in America.

A second highly significant Brennan opinion is the leading case on obscenity. Obscenity is a form of speech or press, but until Brennan wrote there had never been a decision by the Court as to whether or not this kind of speech or publication is protected by the First Amendment to the Constitution. Brennan held that it was not, that the Constitution gives no protection to obscene publications.

In this leading case, Brennan opened, but by no means finished, a large and difficult subject. It remained to determine just what is obscene, and so subject to prohibition. The effort to answer this second question must be regarded as one of the Court's least outstanding accomplishments of the past several years; indeed, as a stroll along New York's Forty-second Street or equivalent walks in other cities will quickly illustrate, it would appear at the moment that, though obscenity may be prohibited under the Brennan opinion, nothing qualifies as obscene. It may be expected that Brennan will have something further to say on this subject another time.

A third truly major opinion by Brennan was the *Du Pont-General Motors* case requiring Du Pont to sell its General Motors holdings because of monopolistic tendencies. This severs the largest corporate combination in America.

What emerges from the Brennan opinions is a positively startling personality combination. When he is at the business of judging, nothing is more deceiving, as the Des Moines paper had said at the time of his appointment, than the impression that this is simply a jolly, slightly portly Irishman with a happy-go-lucky approach. The happy Irishman turns out to have an absolutely fearless mind. The greatest terror for a human being is oftentimes a new idea, but Brennan is absolutely unafraid. He is a man for whom it is never enough to say, "We have always done it this way."

His whole judicial philosophy is caught up in the phrase quoted earlier from the New Jersey Supreme Court opinion dealing with the right of the defendant to see his own confession. "My sense of justice," says Brennan, "requires a particular result." Brennan's is a keenly edged sense of justice and, within deeply respected constitutional limitations, it cuts through the case to its result. There has been no one on the Court quite like Brennan since the Court's preceding Irishman, Justice Frank Murphy. Murphy, too, was prepared to go where his sense of justice led him. The difference is that Brennan combines with his natural law philosophy a greater skill in dealing with legal materials. He knows not only where he wants to go, but how to get there.

What is striking about the Brennan opinions is his willingness to make changes. When he was barely on the Court, in the matter of the servicemen's dependents, Brennan altered the result. His obscenity opinion is the first to lay out the basic lines of the relationship of obscenity to freedom of speech. His *Du Pont-General Motors* case caused the biggest business separation in American history, at least since Standard Oil was divided. His *Jencks* opinion opened a new chapter in criminal procedure. The apportionment case starts a major reorganization in American government. Novelty invigorates, it never frightens him. One can almost feel the zest in the first sentence of his 1964 opinion on the alleged libel of a Birmingham, Alabama, police commissioner by *The New York Times:* "We are required for the first time in this case to determine the extent to which the constitutional protections for speech and press limit a State's power to award damages in a libel action brought by a public official against critics of his official conduct."

For purposes of understanding Justice Brennan, perhaps the most revealing opinion he has written was a 1963 dissent. The case is of no particular importance by itself, but it gives a keen insight into Brennan. The substance is that the plaintiff was served with a subpoena to appear before the Un-American Activities Committee of the House of Representatives. We may assume for the purposes of the case that this subpoena was issued and served by a completely unauthorized employee of the Committee, who had no proper power to issue it at all. The plaintiff sued the man who caused the service, claiming that the mere service of the subpoena suggested to his employer that there must be something wrong with him and that, as a result, he lost his job.

A majority of the Court concluded that the plaintiff must lose his case, that Congress had passed no law permitting a court to give damages for abuse of the subpoena power, and that, therefore, there was no jurisdiction in the federal court. This did not satisfy Brennan. He believed that the case raised "novel and important questions" which needed further consideration. He proceeded to develop several theories under which a federal court might be able to act in this case.

An indicative phrase introduces one of these theories: "The second possible theory builds from" a certain earlier decision, he said. Brennan has a builder's mind. Most court cases are decided by a consideration of the applicability to the present case of some past decision. For the mechanical judge, the business of judging is to find that previous case, and once the judge has found a case which seems to be about the same, the process of decision is over. But the creative judge treats the earlier case not as the end of the road but as its beginning; he starts—he builds—from the earlier decision to form a rule of law which will fit the modern situation.

In this little opinion, Brennan is almost thinking out loud as he fumbles through the dark of the authorities for a light on the immediate case. "The matter is not free from doubt," he says; he is not ready to make up his mind. By the time Brennan was done, he had taken what seems superficially to be a simple matter and revealed it as genuinely complicated. The very heart of his approach to any problem is found in one sentence: "This Court," he says, is not "helpless to inaugurate in the federal courts" the sound principle that a Government officer who uses his power for some personal purpose of his own shall pay for it.

That is it. Brennan is never afraid to inaugurate. He may fumble and flounder for an answer; as he says in this opinion, "I am not prepared to offer definitive solutions." But while a blessed humility may keep him from making quick answers to all of the hard problems of life, he is never unwilling to ask himself the truly hard questions.

One final illustration suggests other qualities of Brennan's work. In the 1963 school-prayer case, the opinion of the Court is some twenty pages long. With it is a seventy-six-page individual concurrence by Justice Brennan, which is the most thorough canvassing of the problems of church and state in the Supreme Court records. An opinion so large is scarcely simply to be read—it must be scaled, like a good-sized mountain, and different qualities will be found at different levels. The most conspicuous single quality is Brennan's personal loyalty to the Court and the Constitution, and his willingness to stand up and be counted in favor of both. We are told in the Bible that Jesus told the people the prayer that they should say, and yet the Court held that the public schools were not the place to say it. Brennan is a good Catholic, one active in the affairs of his church and devoted to its teachings. He knew many Catholics could be expected to be hostile to the Court's result; and he knew, also, that for many of them, his personal view would be of consequence. He desired to put their minds at ease, saying "The principles which we reaffirm and apply today can hardly be thought novel or radical. They are, in truth, as old as the Republic itself, and have always been as integral a part of the First Amendment as the very words of that charter of religious liberty."

Brennan was thus taking his basic stand with his fellow Justices, while he reassured his fellow countrymen in general and his fellow Catholics in particular. But he is not a man to give conclusions only. He explored the detailed lessons of history concerning the purposes of the constitutional Amendment, but not for the purpose of being confined by that history. He recognized that Jefferson and Madison could not have had this precise problem in mind; the Amendment is older by many years than the public school system. Rather, he thought, his duty was to determine the basic purposes or objectives they had in mind, and to test the current action by those objectives.

Passing the history of the Amendment itself, Brennan ascended the pathway of the past to the decisions of the Supreme Court, reviewing all of the leading cases. Then he brought this historical learning to bear on the particular cases before the Court, studying each of the arguments and then moving on to consider each of the other basic problems of the church-state relationship in our own time as they might relate to these cases. The result is an opinion which, while it purports to give only Brennan's conclusions, will help many another American make up his own mind.

These immense opinions can only be done by tremendous hard work. The Justice's usual work schedule is from about eight in the mornings to six in the evenings, six days a week; and on Sundays, he studies papers at home. He is a convivial fellow and a good after-dinner speaker, enjoying such affairs. Moreover, like Justice Clark, he is deeply interested in judicial administration, and he would like nothing better than to be able to go about the country as Clark does to meet judges and lawyers locally on these problems. But he puts an extremely tight rein on himself, realizing that for the kind of work he wants to do he must give every possible minute to the business of judging. As a result, he limits public appearances outside the Court during the term to one a year, and some years he eliminates them altogether. His occasional appearances are usually on matters of practice and particularly on criminal procedure. One measure of how hard he works will be seen by anyone who visits with him early in the morning and again late in the afternoon of the same day. In the morning he will be full of bounce, energy, and verve. By day's end he is clearly tired all through. In the summertime Brennan picks up his bar duties. For five years he has participated in the New York University summer training program for state supreme court judges, programs widely regarded as extremely valuable by those judges. For two years he has been captain of an American group of lawyers and judges which, with their opposite numbers in England, have met to discover what English and American ways of justice can be used to advantage by the other.

Within his own office, Brennan divides the petitions for certiorari, applications to be heard, between the clerks and himself; in any given week these are worked up by whichever happens to be least busy at the moment. On his opinions, his clerks prepare a first draft for him.

Brennan speaks with an almost envying, though highly good-natured, admiration of Justices like Black and Douglas who can work more quickly than he. So far as he personally is concerned, he finds that he writes slowly, and he perfectly happily accepts all the help he can get.

His opinion-writing process is this: first, he calls in the particular clerk to whom he is going to assign the particular case. He gives that clerk general oral instructions as to how the draft should go. The clerk then does a draft, which is returned to the Justice. He tells the clerks to give him everything—he would rather make the cuts himself than find something missing. In a particular instance, a clerk gave him a thirty-page first draft with eleven pages of footnotes. Thereupon, the Justice spent four solid days, including the bulk of a Sunday, working over the draft. His draft differed from the draft which his clerk had given him in that in the first place it was only thirteen pages long and had only three pages of notes. In the second place, and rather more important, it reached a result exactly opposite from the clerk's. Brennan drastically revises in every case, and what emerges from the office is unquestionably his. However, he cheerfully acknowledges that he has no pride of opinion or pride of authorship and anyone in the office who can turn out a good paragraph will have a fair chance of seeing it used.

Because Brennan has a real interest in judicial administration, he gives close thought to how the Court can keep abreast of ever-increasing work. The Court is currently giving much time to superintendence of administration of the criminal law in the various states. Brennan hopes that the Court has by now made sufficiently clear what the Constitution demands of the states by way of fair trials and that the states will be able to dispose of these problems in the future with less and less federal supervision. A second area of potential improvement is in the antitrust field. Under a special provision of law, the Department of Justice is now able to bring many of these cases directly from the trial courts to the Supreme Court. Brennan believes that these cases probably consume more time than they are worth. The situation would improve if the Department could be persuaded to let more of these cases go to the other courts.

Brennan and his wife lead simple lives with a minimum of social ostentation. They take a keen interest in the progress of their three children, the older two of whom have chosen law as a career, while the third, a girl, is very much an enthusiastic father's darling.

His work for the rest of his life is cut out for him. It is the work he most believes in, the work of preserving, protecting, and if need be even enlarging the liberties of American citizens.

In performing this work, Brennan will never be timid. He believes that the courts must carry their full load in securing a climate of freedom. He approaches his work with a happy confidence in America. "As for the country," he says, "I read that we are too fat and complacent, but I just don't believe it. When I see such ventures as the Peace Corps and when I listen to my children and their friends, I see how unafraid our youngsters are, how well informed they are, how willing to face the future. If I have a concern, it is that there is not enough education in our American ideals. There is too much talk of the evils of Communism and not enough teaching about how great and wonderful our own system is. I favor training in science and math, but let us not forget the need of education in the meaning of such concepts as liberty, freedom, and self-restraint, which are the glory of America."

Brennan will do his best to tell America what liberty, freedom, and self-restraint mean.

© Karsh of Ottawa 1964

© Karsh of Ottawa 1964

Chapter Eight

MR. JUSTICE
Potter Stewart

THE WORLD WAR II generation are those Americans who came to their maturity during the war years and who developed their careers after it. This World War II generation has been duly described, as are all generations, as terrible. It includes more than its share of the fast-buck boys, the men of cheap morality, the generation building lives around endless television, nominal reading, and the insatiable pursuit of indulgence. It is the generation of tail-fin automobiles as a symbol of Americanism, the time of disassociation from community problems by the flight to the suburbs.

The World War II generation is all these things; it may be terrible. But it is also great. It is a get-things-done generation, a generation which overthrew Hitler, Hirohito, and Mussolini, a generation which includes the astronauts and the men who lifted them into space, the generation of young men in politics like John Kennedy and William Scranton, and in medicine like Jonas Salk. It is the generation which in business and in government is taking over America.

Potter Stewart is the first man of this World War II generation to come to the Supreme Court of the United States. When he went to the Court in 1958, he was only forty-three years of age. He is youth coming into power, and he represents the most highly esteemed qualities of the modern man. He is in astonishing degree competent, temperate, urbane, and sophisticated in his outlook. He is technically completely well trained for the position he holds, and his product has high gloss and perfect finish.

This quality of being a representative of his time reaches the very being of Stewart. For example, this is an era which knows no servants. Stewart doesn't do it often, but he can push his own lawn mower and he knows how to get the grocery cart around the supermarket. It is a generation in which, while family ties are crumbling in extraordinary degree, some very typical families manage to maintain security, solidarity, and intimate companionship. The Stewart family companionship has these qualities. Mrs. Stewart, an exceptionally attractive woman of unostentatious but excellent style, is very likely to turn up in the Supreme Court guest seats to smile affectionately when her husband is handing down an opinion, and the Justice will spend much time playing baseball or fishing with his teen-age sons, Potter, Jr., and David, or in the company of his daughter Harriet.

Stewart came to the law via a far more comfortable passageway than many of his older colleagues. The parents of the World War II generation had time to become comfortable themselves and to send their children to school in style. Stewart comes from a Cincinnati family; he was born in Jackson, Michigan, on January 23, 1915, only because his mother happened to be vacationing there at the time. His father was then a Cincinnati lawyer.

Stewart had his preparatory education at the Hotchkiss School in Lakeville, Connecticut, and then went to Yale College. In both Hotchkiss and Yale College his good work earned him academic scholarships. At Yale, he majored in English literature and was chairman of the *Yale Daily News* (which he put on a solid New Deal line), and he was graduated with Phi Beta Kappa honors.

Stewart never seriously considered being anything but a lawyer. He spent a couple of summers on the Cincinnati *Times-Star,* and when he was graduated from Yale he toyed with the possibility of going into newspaper work, but the notion passed before it ever hardened into even serious impulse. In 1938 he went to Cambridge University in England where he studied international law and then came back to the Yale Law School from 1938 to 1941. His law school experience was a well-rounded success. He won the school's competition for making the best oral argument, had a post of consequence on the school's legal publication, and graduated *cum laude*. Upon graduation he duly went to a distinguished New York law firm for a year.

The war broke a pattern which was on its way to becoming a fur-lined rut. The story is typical. Lad of good opportunity and good family from the hinterland comes east to prep school, college, and law school; does well; goes to Wall Street and then becomes very rich, very influential in the business world, and a member of a flossy series of clubs. If Stewart had stuck to the pattern, he would today have been very prosperous, very significant, and very unknown. But the pattern began to break with the war. He went into the Navy as a lieutenant and had a typical "Mr. Roberts" experience. His own description of his service, which was predominantly on oil tankers serving in the Atlantic and the Mediterranean, was that he was "floating around on a sea of 100 octane gas, bored to death 99 per cent of the time and scared to death 1 per cent." He was in what he called the dungaree Navy rather than the uniformed Navy. While the service was tedious, it was that peculiar kind of tedium which comes of constantly living with frightful danger. Since he was engaged in hauling petroleum, there was always a danger of submarines, and there could be no rescue after a hit. A sister ship was torpedoed and sunk within a few hundred yards of his own vessel on one voyage. He came out of the service with three battle stars.

Upon his release from service, Stewart returned to his New York office for a time, but then he made his big move and went back to Cincinnati. There he became a member of a great firm of that city and began to take an interest in local public affairs.

Politics was never a primary interest for Stewart. His father had been mayor of Cincinnati from 1938 to 1947, and then became a member of the Ohio Supreme Court. In 1949, Justice Stewart began the first of two terms on the Cincinnati City Council. In 1952 and 1953 he was vice-mayor, the highest office he ever held before becoming a judge.

Meanwhile, his personal politics had settled along the line of what is generally described today as "modern Republicanism." He knew and deeply respected Senator Taft, Cincinnati's leading figure in the public life. Senator Bricker, Ohio's other Republican Senator, he knew only casually.

The crisis for moderate Ohio Republicans came prior to the Republican convention of 1952, when the opposing candidates were Taft and Eisenhower. All Stewart's personal loyalties attracted him to Taft; but Stewart could not persuade himself that Taft was what the country needed. He felt that Taft, whom he greatly admired, was a great legislator but that he might be a poor executive. He believed that Taft had a particularly poor sense of appointment; some of the persons he used in his campaign were particularly glaring examples of this to Stewart. He did not need to be involved in the preconvention tussle. After Eisenhower was nominated, Stewart was active in southern Ohio, particularly in carrying on organizational work which could pull the Taft and Eisenhower men together and soften the bitterness of the time.

In 1954, President Eisenhower appointed Stewart to the United States Court of Appeals for the Sixth Circuit. This is a federal appeals court for the states of Michigan, Ohio, Kentucky, and Tennessee. As is likely to be the case in such an appointment, the circumstances were a combination of a good deal of merit and a good deal of luck.

A vacancy arose because of the retirement of a judge with the improbable name of Xenophon Hicks, of Tennessee, during the latter portion of the Truman Administration. President Truman did not get around to filling the vacancy, and it was thus left for the Eisenhower Administration, which concluded to give the seat to Ohio. Appointments to such seats are predominantly the prerogative of the Senator or Senators from the state who are members of the party in power, and as between Senators Bricker and Taft it had been settled that this would be a Taft appointment. Taft's first selection was a very able man but one who was slightly over the age of sixty. President Eisenhower and his Attorney General, Herbert Brownell, had an ironclad rule that no one over sixty would be appointed to any Court of Appeals, and they refused the choice on this ground. Taft was unable to make a satisfactory second choice.

Stewart's father was at this time a member of the Supreme Court of Ohio. One day he met the probate judge, Chase Davies, an influential political figure in Cincinnati. Judge Davies discussed with Stewart's father the problem of filling the Sixth Circuit vacancy and suggested that Potter would be very acceptable. He was in doubt, however, as to whether the future Justice would be interested. Local Republican leaders had recently tried to induce Stewart to go either for the Republican nomination for Congress or for Lieutenant Governor. Stewart had concluded not to try because he wanted to stick to his law practice once his service on the city council was terminated. The group put it up to the Justice's father to ask his son how he felt about the appointment, with the understanding that if he were interested, they would all recommend him to Taft.

That afternoon, the father called his son to say that he ought to consider whether he would wish to go to the Court of Appeals if he could because there was a real chance that he might have the appointment if he wanted it. Stewart spent the weekend in a genuine soul-searching with his wife as to whether he was ready to take a step at an age, thirty-nine, which would take him out of active practice for the rest of his life. It was a genuinely hard decision to make, but by Monday morning he and his wife had decided, and he reported back that if he could have the post he would like it. According to Attorney General Brownell, who has told the story several times, Senator Taft thereupon called the Attorney General, said, "All right, this time I have one that is young enough for you," and offered him the thirty-nine-year-old Stewart. However, this tale is almost certainly apocryphal because Taft died before the Circuit appointment and probably before a decision concerning it was made.

In four years on the Sixth Circuit Court of Appeals, Stewart wrote

on many subjects. At the time of his appointment to the Supreme
Court, one of America's most able analysts of judicial work studied
Stewart's performance on the Court of Appeals, concluding that
Stewart's primary concern was that the law should be fair, that decisions should reach sensible results. He predicted that Stewart's primary achievement would be to leave the world of the law more orderly
than he found it. Two of the most colorful of Stewart's cases during
the Court of Appeals years will illustrate his approach.

The best known Stewart decision was probably the 1956 segregation case. The case arose from Hillsboro, Ohio, a community which
had three elementary schools. Two of these had for many years been
attended by white students only, and the third by Negro students only.
Ohio law precludes segregation, and the high school and seventh and
eighth grades had been desegregated. In 1954 the town set up a system
of zones, providing that the students from two disconnected remote
zones would attend the Negro school. At the same time it set out to
build enlarged schools upon the completion of which, it was said, the
town intended to abandon segregation altogether.

The validity of this system was brought to the Court of Appeals,
which two to one held that the scheme was illegal. By hindsight this is
perfectly obvious; enough cases were later decided that the matter is
no longer doubtful. But in 1956 this was not so. Then the path of desegregation was only beginning to unfold, and the case was by no
means easy. The two majority judges, of whom Stewart was one,
agreed on the principle, differing a little as to the nature of the order.
The views of Judge Stewart, which finally became the order of the
Court, were that from the day of the decision forward, any new Negro
students seeking to go to school in Hillsboro should be admitted on an
unsegregated basis. Those in the existing segregated schools should
be treated on an unsegregated basis by the beginning of the fall term
in the year in which the decision was made. To the argument that
this might have the effect of crowding the classrooms, Stewart observed, "Overcrowded classrooms, however, are unfortunately not

peculiar to Hillsboro, and the avoidance alone of somewhat over-crowded classrooms cannot justify segregation of school children solely because of the color of their skins."

The opinion reflects the mixture of respect for authority and practical sense which are the two key elements of Stewart's mental makeup. On the one hand, the Supreme Court had said that segregation was to be ended with "all deliberate speed." Stewart said: "The Board's action was, therefore, not only entirely unsupported by any color of State law, but in knowing violation of the Constitution of the United States. The Board's subjective purpose was no doubt, and understandably, to reflect the 'spirit of the community' and avoid 'racial problems,' as testified by the Superintendent of Schools. But the law of Ohio and the Constitution of the United States simply left no room for the Board's action, whatever motives the Board may have had."

On the other hand, the case came on for decision in the middle of a school year. Stewart said:

Our decision in this case will be announced in the midst of a school year. No reason appears why those Negro children of school age who are not now attending any school should not be admitted immediately to whichever of the three schools a system of attendance zones based upon geographic or other relevant nonracial considerations may dictate. To undertake before the end of the present school year a wholesale shifting of the other Negro and white children now in school might, however, serve to cause dislocation and hardship out of proportion to the purpose to be served.

A second well known Stewart opinion was his dissent in a case involving the conviction of a Negro named Henderson by a Michigan court for the offense of rape. Sometimes the law is too slow. No such complaint could be made of the law in this case. As Stewart summarized the facts:

Late in the afternoon of August 5, 1942, James Henderson learned from a friend that the police of Mount Clemens, Michigan, were looking for him in connection with an alleged rape that had occurred a few days earlier. He went to the office of the state police, identified himself, and was taken into custody. About 7:30 that evening, he was turned over to the Mount Clemens police, and about 8:30 P.M. was delivered by them to the Mount Clemens jail. Two and a half hours later he had been sentenced to prison for the rest of his life.

Henderson had no lawyer. He signed a confession at 9:30 P.M. At 10:20 P.M., a special court session was called. With no one in the courtroom except the judge, the prosecutor, the defendant, and the police, he was quickly convicted and sentenced. "The motivation" for these speedy proceedings in "the nighttime," said Stewart, "seems clearly to have been fear of possible mob violence." Stewart thought that certainly a lawyer was needed to protect Henderson's rights. He analyzed the difficulty of proving rape under the law of Michigan, and showed that there was not even present a prosecuting witness to testify as to what Henderson might have done. It seemed to him a clear case in which a lawyer was necessary.

In 1958, Justice Harold Burton retired from the Supreme Court. Burton, who had been former mayor of Cleveland and United States Senator from Ohio, left a vacancy which could be regarded as one to be filled by an appointee from one of the Sixth Circuit states. The President was not required to choose someone from this area, but it was certainly a reasonable first place to look. Of the Court of Appeals judges for the Sixth Circuit, Stewart was quite clearly the only serious one eligible; for while he may have been a little young for the office, the others were a little old.

Attorney General William Rogers called Stewart and asked him to come in to Washington for a discussion. At the time of the call, the Burton retirement was not yet announced, so that Stewart as he traveled was at a loss as to why he was wanted. However, upon arrival the Burton story was in the papers and, as Stewart has said: "Suddenly I had an idea why I had been called to Washington. It knocked the wind out of me, just the idea." Shortly thereafter Rogers reached Stewart in Washington, and told him the President wanted to see him at eight the next morning. At the morning meeting, President Eisenhower told Stewart of his selection and the appointment was announced that afternoon, October 14, 1958.

Stewart had the burden of serving for seven months as a recess appointee to the Court before he was confirmed on May 5, 1959. The confirmation was contested, primarily because of Stewart's part in the Hillsboro School case. While there was never much doubt that he would be confirmed, the question was nominally in issue, and he had to conduct himself as a Supreme Court Justice with the question of continuity hanging over his head.

The recess appointment problem is by no means unique to Stewart; President Eisenhower faced the same difficulty when he appointed Chief Justice Warren and Justice Brennan. Of the hundred Justices, fourteen had been appointed in recess and were confirmed many months later, and a fifteenth, John Rutledge, of South Carolina, served for a year in 1795 as Chief Justice of the United States and then his appointment was rejected. The practice has seemed undesirable to many, and the Stewart appointment has been cited as an extreme instance. Stewart participated in a case during this pendency period, which especially raised comment; it was a difficult problem of search and seizure. The Court, five to four, with Justice Stewart in the majority, upheld the right to search a Baltimore home for an alleged violation of a health ordinance, the search being made without a warrant. A *New York Times* columnist made some issue of the undesirability of having decisions on such important matters in the circumstances.

On the other hand, if Presidents did not make recess appointments, the Court might fall far behind in its work. All these problems disappeared, as they usually do, because Stewart was confirmed. When Stewart came before the Senate Judiciary hearing for his confirmation hearing, his Hillsboro School opinion led to much questioning by southern Senators. He made forthrightly clear that he had no intention of going to the Supreme Court for the purpose of undercutting its segregation decisions. As a result, Senators Johnston of South Carolina and Eastland of Mississippi dissented from the Committee report in his favor. The Hillsboro School case and the Michigan rape case, discussed above, were also discussed critically on the Senate floor by these Senators and Senator Strom Thurmond of South Carolina. Nevertheless, he was confirmed handily.

The keen sense of fair trial exhibited by Stewart on the lower court is also illustrated in a 1963 decision which will serve as a model of Stewart's method in a simple case. The defendant was charged with having robbed a bank in Lake Charles, Louisiana, kidnapping three employees, and killing one of them. A few hours later, he was arrested and the next morning was interviewed by the sheriff in the course of which he admitted the offenses. This interview was filmed, and the film was broadcast over a local television station for three consecutive days, in the course of which it was seen by up to two-thirds of the population of the community. The defendant was duly convicted by a jury which included three persons who had seen the television show and which also included two deputy sheriffs. The issue before the Supreme Court was whether, under the Constitution, the defendant was entitled to have his trial in some county in which the film had not been televised.

Justice Stewart, for a unanimous Court, said he was entitled to trial in a community which had not seen the film:

> For anyone who has ever watched television the conclusion cannot be avoided that this spectacle, to the tens of thousands of people who saw and heard it, in a very real sense *was* [the] trial. . . . Any subsequent court proceedings in a community so pervasively exposed to such a spectacle could be but a hollow formality.

The defendant, whether he was guilty or not, had a right to a lawyer to defend him, to plead not guilty, and to be tried in a courtroom presided over by a judge and not in a jail presided over by a sheriff.

In the particular instance, the defendant may very well be guilty, in which case he can be found so on retrial. But a practice of televised advance trials in this fashion clearly would make a mockery of the law, and not much needs to be said about it. What needs to be noted for the purpose of understanding Stewart is that not much *was* said about it. Men, and particularly judges, are given abundant opportunities to be brief, but these are opportunities of which all too few can take advantage. Stewart's opinion is four pages long—perhaps twelve hundred words. For Stewart is a man who, when he has not much to say, does not say it.

Other cases on highly technical matters will illustrate this Stewart talent. The defendants were a New Mexico newspaper and a New Mexico radio station so located near the Texas border that some of their circulation or audience was in each state. Certain advertising was legal under the law of Texas but illegal under the law of New Mexico. The issue was whether the New Mexico law could apply to this interstate advertising or whether this New Mexico law was improperly interfering with interstate commerce. The Stewart decision held that the New Mexico law could apply.

The opinion, a model of brevity, runs some eight pages. The first paragraph states the problem, the second states the New Mexico law, and the third states what had happened in the proceedings thus far. Stewart decides the principal issue in three paragraphs which bring out whatever needs to be known about the leading previous decisions. Another few paragraphs dispose of the only other issue.

Another illustration of this faculty for clear, concise directness is a December, 1963, decision. The case presented one of the knottiest technical problems in the law. Certain land was along the Missouri River which makes the border between the states of Nebraska and Missouri. When the river shifts, since it is the border, under one rule of law the land might shift with it, passing back and forth between the two states. A case involving ownership of the land arose which required a decision as to which state it was in. A Nebraska court, holding that the land was in Nebraska, made a decision concerning who owned it. But the Nebraska court had the power to make such a decision only if the land in truth was in Nebraska—if it was in Missouri, a Nebraska court would have no jurisdiction over it. The loser therefore took the very same question to the courts of Missouri and started all over again. The question was, when land is on the edge of a shifting river which makes a border between two states, is the decision of the state which first decides in which state the land lies binding upon the other?

There is no profit in going further into this complicated problem. The case is chosen to illustrate that, along with the high-flown matters of great policy, there are also hard, knotty, precise technical questions of law to be decided by the Supreme Court. The Stewart decision in the Missouri River case is really a model of a decision on a point of this kind. No one is likely to be confused about the law of this subject in the future; no one is going to doubt just what the Court has said; and no one is likely to be dissatisfied either with the reasoning or the result. This is not a great sparkling diamond of a case, it is simply a nice little jewel; and in work of this kind, Stewart is extremely good.

One reason that Stewart's opinions have such a quality of fine etching is that he etches them. That is to say, he usually works his opinions out longhand, coping with each word and each detail as he does it the first time. There are basically two very different styles, the one being the write-and-revise-over-and-over-again style and the other the do-it-slowly-and-carefully-the-first-time style. Each has its merits and each is suited to different personalities. The meticulous word-at-a-time style is particularly suited to Stewart. The great enemy of judicial brevity is usually dictation; with modern dictating devices, it is so appallingly easy to run on! Justice Black is one of the few Justices who can both dictate and be concise, and this is because he steels himself to sand down each paragraph of his dictated product before he is done. One reason that opinions were shorter in ages long gone is the sheer burden on the Justice who had to write them himself; and Stewart is a happy throwback to this earlier day. A 1964 opinion holding that a man's hotel room is not subject to search without a warrant merely because a hotel clerk consents to it illustrates this brevity; the defendant is out of court, out of the hotel, and out of jail in about fifteen hundred words of Stewart text.

The fine polish Stewart puts on his technical matters makes him all the more effective when he hits the colorful big cases. The one area in which Stewart has been basically at odds with the rest of the Court is on the permissibility of school prayers. In 1962 the Court held, over the dissent of Stewart, that the schools of New York could not begin each day's classes with a prayer. The text of his opinion is so short that the general flavor of it can easily be set out here. Stewart says: "I cannot see how an 'official religion' is established by letting those who want to say a prayer say it. On the contrary, I think that to deny the wish of these school children to join in reciting this prayer is to deny them the opportunity of sharing in the spiritual heritage of our nation. ... What is relevant to the issue here is not the history of an established church in sixteenth century England or eighteenth century America, but the history of the religious traditions of our people, reflected in countless practices of the institutions and officials of our Government."

Stewart noted that the Supreme Court and both houses of Congress begin their sessions with an appeal to God and that all Presidents begin their terms of office in the same way. He pointed out that the national anthem, the pledge of allegiance, and the coins all have invocations to the Lord. He concluded that all New York had done was "to recognize and to follow the deeply entrenched and highly cherished spiritual traditions of our nation—traditions which come down to us from those who almost 200 years ago avowed their 'firm reliance on the protection of divine Providence' when they proclaimed the freedom and independence of this brave new world."

For all its brief eloquence, the Stewart opinion is open to the charge that it is aside from the main point. No one has to be a Congressman, no one has to be on the Supreme Court, no one has to be President; but the laws require that the children go to school. The real issue, therefore, is whether they are under compulsion, either direct or indirect, to engage in religious activities which are not of their own choosing. Stewart himself apparently realized that this phase of the problem needed further attention, and he turned to it when the next school-prayer case came up again in 1963.

The issue in this second case was whether Bible readings or the Lord's Prayer could be required as an exercise at beginning of school in Pennsylvania. Once again, eight Justices thought that this was improper in the schools, and again Stewart was the only dissenter. But in this case he agreed with the other Justices that if there were any elements of coercion forcing students to participate in these exercises, then the activity would be "clearly" improper. He asked only that further evidence be taken on the issue of whether there was in fact any such coercion. He said, "What our Constitution indispensably protects is the freedom of each of us, be he Jew or Agnostic, Christian or Atheist, Buddhist or Free Thinker, to believe or disbelieve, to worship or not worship, to pray or keep silent, according to his own conscience, uncoerced and unrestrained by Government." He said:

* * * a law which provided for religious exercises during the school day and which contained no excusal provision would obviously be unconstitutionally coercive upon those who did not wish to participate. And even under a law containing an excusal provision, if the exercises were held during the school day, and no equally desirable alternative were provided by the school authorities, the likelihood that children might be under at least some psychological compulsion to participate would be great.

A Stewart opinion attracting some attention was the case of the movie *Lady Chatterley's Lover*. The current wave of sex-oriented publications and movies makes Lady Chatterley appear relatively chaste, but she and her friend the gamekeeper were an advance guard for promiscuity for many years, and when her adventures were converted into a movie, New York refused to license the distribution of the film on the ground of the immorality of certain of its scenes. The final reviewing authority took the view that "the whole theme of this motion picture is immoral," because it presents "adultery as a desirable, acceptable and proper pattern of behavior." The New York Court of

Appeals unanimously found that the movie was not obscene in the activities displayed but that it was not to be licensed because it "portrays adultery as proper behavior."

This is the kind of problem which pushes a man to the ultimates of his values. Justice Stewart's personal moral values are strict. At the same time, he does not conceive it to be his job to legislate his own moral values into the Constitution; and the First Amendment gives great freedom for the advocacy of ideas whether Mr. Justice Stewart happens to like them or not. In holding the state law invalid, he said:

It is contended that the State's action was justified because the motion picture attractively portrays a relationship which is contrary to the moral standards, the religious precepts, and the legal code of its citizenry. This argument misconceives what it is that the Constitution protects. Its guarantee is not confined to the expression of ideas that are conventional or shared by a majority. It protects advocacy of the opinion that adultery may sometimes be proper, no less than advocacy of socialism or the single tax. And in the realm of ideas it protects expression which is eloquent no less than that which is unconvincing.

Justice Stewart is a man to tend to his knitting. He makes very few outside appearances, commonly working at night and on the weekends at home. The Washington social whirl has no keen attraction for the Stewarts; the big party life they leave to others. He regards his job as an intensely personal one, in which the duty of decision on every detail is his and his alone, and he is particularly careful with facts, with a habit of interrupting himself even in fairly casual conversation to check to make sure that what he is saying is correct. He admires the work that Justice Clark does for the full Court in participating in Bar activities around the country, but for himself, he finds his work so time-consuming that much as he would like to do the same thing, it will probably be years, if ever, before he will feel free to do so. This is not because of any extreme personal reserve—he is warmly cordial with all, and thoroughly candid in occasional interviews. But he is a man with a single job to do and a strong determination to do it.

As his work on the lower court showed, Stewart is determined that justice should be fair to the poor. He may be assumed to have been delighted in joining in the final decision in 1963 which declared it to be the duty of every state to ensure that all criminal defendants should have lawyers available to them. He feels that there is no goal more worthy than attempting to provide the same justice for the poor as for the rich.

While Stewart is mentally extremely quick, he is careful in making up his mind. Hence oral arguments of cases have somewhat less persuasiveness with him than with some of the other Justices. He appreciates the oral arguments, realizing that sometimes they have a force which the written briefs filed in every case may lack. However, on the technical matters, he feels that the decision depends on matters of detail which cannot well be explained orally and which require close, time-consuming work.

The social movement of the time which Stewart can most easily accept and join is desegregation. In one of his rare speeches he has expressed the anticipation that the pace of desegregation will be accelerated. He finds great progress in the border states areas since the leading decision of 1954. Kentucky was in his old circuit and is across the river from his old home and he knows full well how much progress has been made there. However, he finds that "distressingly little" progress has been made in other areas and is sympathetic with the feeling of those who think that the progress of desegregation is moving too slowly.

In the summer of 1959, at an American Bar Association meeting in Miami, in a sailfish-catching foray, Stewart was the only bar member who landed his fish, getting one almost eight feet long. The incident is typical; he is a man who lands his fish, who gets the job done. The World War II generation may have a sense of cheerful contentment that its first representative on the United States Supreme Court is the kind of man it would want: moderate, temperate, incisive, effective. Potter Stewart is no legal revolutionary bent on materially changing the system he has found; he will increase the order and clarity of that system and make it more fair.

© Karsh of Ottawa 1964

Chapter Nine

MR. JUSTICE
Byron R. White

THE TIME was May, 1961. The Kennedy Administration had been in office for less than six months, and the Department of Justice under Attorney General Robert Kennedy was just shaking down into a working machine. A group of Freedom Riders, as they named themselves, left Washington, D.C., determined to cross the southeastern United States by bus without having Negroes seated from the back and whites seated from the front as was required by the segregation laws of that region.

The first integrated buses reached Alabama in mid-May. There one of them was destroyed by fire and a dozen persons were injured. The Freedom Riders progressed to Birmingham, where, after street fighting, the effort was, for the moment, abandoned.

A few days later an integrated passenger load moved through Alabama from Birmingham to Montgomery. Here the gathering crowds became a hostile mob. When Deputy Attorney General Byron White, second ranking officer of the Department of Justice, returned from lunch on one of these days, he discovered that a Department of Justice officer in Montgomery had been injured in a riot. Quickly arranging for a turbojet from the Civil Aeronautics Administration, White gathered an Assistant Attorney General who was a native of Alabama, his secretary, a personal assistant; grabbed an armload of books; and headed for Montgomery. On the way down, White dictated papers necessary for court applications to restrain the outbreaks. On arrival he took charge of the small army of United States marshals and set out to restore order in Montgomery.

This was a time of tensions, but White is a man of calm. He rarely talks more than he needs to, and when, in a confrontation with the Governor of Alabama, the Governor asked, "Where are all those Freedom Riders?" White dryly replied that they were in the hospitals to which the Governor's men had sent them.

With peace restored, White went back to his desk in the Department of Justice. It was unlike him to take so personal a hold of the situation; this had been an emergency and he had had no choice. Basically he and the Attorney General ran the Department through a first-class staff largely recruited by White.

When Byron White was appointed to the Supreme Court on March 30, 1962, he was not yet forty-five years of age. Yet President Kennedy was able to say of this Westerner whom the President had known for over twenty years, "His character, experience and intellectual force qualify him superbly for service on the nation's highest tribunal. He has excelled in everything he has attempted—in his academic life, in his military service, in his career before the Bar, and in the federal government." The statement was precisely true.

White was born on June 8, 1917, in Colorado and was brought up in the small town of Wellington in that state. His family was certainly not prosperous, and White started earning not only his own spending money but money for the family by working in the sugar beet fields before he was ten years old. He went to school, of course; but the schools of the sugar beet region let out when the kids were needed for the harvest, and they could earn a dollar or two a day. Later he worked as a section hand on a railroad.

White's parents lacked even a high school education, but they wanted something better for their boys. White took an early and keen interest both in his school work and in the sports connected with it. He played football, basketball, baseball and was a track man too. But when it came time to go to college, no one came around to dish out athletic inducements. White earned a scholarship to the state university because he was first in his high school class.

At the university, White became a locally famous student, making Phi Beta Kappa in his junior year, and a nationally famous football player. Before he was done he was the best known scholar-athlete in the country, whether for that or any other period. His football accomplishments were no lucky break. For example, he spent thirty to forty-five minutes a day practicing catching punts at full speed, and his punt returns made immense yardage during the games.

After college White fitted in three seasons of professional football around a stay as a Rhodes Scholar at Oxford. In 1938, he was the highest paid professional football player in the country. There was some talk of his attempting rugby at Oxford, but the English wouldn't let a professional athlete play. The English experience not only gave him some acquaintance with the English and with English law, but gave him an opportunity to tour all over Europe. John F. Kennedy was traveling in Europe that same year, and the two happened to meet several times.

With the start of the war in Europe, White cut off his English education and went to the Yale Law School. He took two years of his law work there before America's entry into the war and finished after it, winning a fine assortment of honors for scholarship. There was a five-year break for military service between his second and his third year in the law school. White has recalled some of his wartime experience in his own words: "Early in the war I was the intelligence officer with the PT boat squadron based on the Solomons, and it was my job to brief the fellows on the intelligence side of their missions before they went out and interview them when they came back and coordinate their missions with the fliers. It was out there that I met Kennedy again, and one of the jobs I had to do was write the report on the accident when his boat was sunk. I remember riding on his boat a couple of times—that is, the boat they gave him after he had lost his first boat. As a result of these encounters with the President, I began to get a strong feeling about what kind of fellow he was. He proved himself to be very intelligent in the way he ran his boat, as well as cool and

151

courageous under fire. I concluded he was a pretty solid sort of person."

On graduation from law school, White went to the Supreme Court as a law clerk for Chief Justice Fred Vinson. From Washington he headed to Denver, joining an excellent medium-sized firm there, built a good practice, and began to take some part in the state's Democratic politics. Early in the Kennedy campaign, White was active in seeking Colorado delegates for Kennedy, and as the campaign moved into full swing, Kennedy asked him to become head of the National Citizens for Kennedy activities. White went to Washington, set up offices, and got to work.

After the election, no one seemed to doubt that White would do something in the administration; he headed everybody's list of eligibles. But there was for a time some doubt as to what his assignment would be. Had Robert Kennedy not become Attorney General, White would have been a natural for this post. When the President finally prevailed on his brother to go into the Department of Justice, White became the Number Two man for the Department.

The combination was ideal because the two men so completely complemented each other. Each has proved cool in judgment, decisive, and scrupulously honest. The Department of Justice holds such great powers that its leadership is inevitably tempted, not so much with vulgar inducements, but with the more delicate persuasions of political advantage for bringing or dismissing this case, making or abstaining from that appointment. White, though young, was an experienced technical lawyer while the Attorney General was instead a first-class policy man with a keen sense of the wishes of his brother, the President.

The first task of the new administration was to recruit senior staff members. This the Attorney General left largely to White. White drew heavily on old Yale associates; it may have been a Harvard administration for the rest of the government, but the colors of the Department of Justice included a thick stripe of Yale blue. The recruitment was White's first great success: Nicholas Katzenbach, who succeeded him as Deputy Attorney General; Lou Oberdorfer, who has run an immensely successful Tax Division without a touch of public criticism; and Burke Marshall, in the Department's hottest spot, the Civil Rights Division, to name only a few.

Not only the Department in Washington, but the Department around the country had to be staffed. Each state has its United States Attorney and their choice inevitably involved a balance of local political considerations with national demands for competence. White's greatest personal success in this regard was Robert Morgenthau, whom he had to fight to get as United States Attorney for New York. Some had doubted that Morgenthau could be tough enough for law enforcement in that rough spot, but his administration proved most successful.

In the internal management of the Department, no one doubted that the ultimate boss was the Attorney General. But Kennedy in turn had great confidence in White and left him with major responsibilities. White took firm hold, asking for daily reports from every division on important matters. The Department is so large and its work so prodigious, running to many thousands of cases, that the various division heads could themselves easily lose track of what was in their divisions. The daily reports not only kept the front office informed but helped to keep the assistants advised as well. White did not run the Department on strictly divisional lines; occasionally he would call in several of the assistants to discuss problems which would then be handled by only one division. Basically the Department officers immediately below him thought of him as a real chief of staff, to whom they could take their substantial questions. He had a way of asking the staff questions to get to the bottom of matters. One senior subordinate recalls that he never asked a question which was not a difficult one; there was no aimless or loose talk in him.

White was quick and his judgment was good and he had the peculiar capacity of being able to bring out the best in the men around him. "If you are working with Byron, your own capacities are multiplied," one of them once said. But while White was quick, he was also careful. Matters were discussed with him as long as necessary to let him make sensible decisions. He decided not only general policy matters but also substantial legal questions, particularly when new fields were being opened. For illustration, a principal drive of the Civil Rights Division was to increase voter registration of Negroes. When there began to be interferences with registration and new legal devices had to be developed to control them, the problems were brought to White to help devise a program. Similarly, when some schools were closed to avoid integration and the problem was thus presented of whether there was a constitutional right to public education, White participated directly in thinking through the legal issues involved.

Rarely has the Department been so free of political influence in the handling of cases as in the Kennedy-White period. The result was probably as pleasing to the Congress as it was to the working staff of the Department. The typical problem is whether a given case shall be prosecuted or not. Someone who is about to be indicted, whether for a claimed antitrust violation, or for nonpayment of taxes, or for some other crime may go to his Congressman or Senator and ask that the Department somehow be pressured not to proceed. Kennedy and White each made so clear that any such pressure would be fruitless that there came to be no attempts. There is not even a substantial rumor that the Department of that period ever folded up for anyone; justice was as even-handed as the staff could make it. Kennedy and White were such effective buffers that no one came to the lower staff looking for favors.

White worked hard at his job, so hard that he was out for a month with genuinely severe digestive troubles. He believes in a stiff administration of justice and thinks that people ought frequently to be better than they sometimes are. As might be expected, he had his quota both of successes and of failures. The Antitrust Division, which had become woefully stale and stodgy over the years, never did reach the level of effectiveness the Attorney General and White wanted, during White's period in the Department. Other phases of the Department's program occasionally dragged. But on the whole the record was one of accomplishment.

White's largest single Department duty was in the appointment of judges. Final decisions on judicial appointments were made by the President, on the recommendation of the Attorney General; but the particular office in the Department which must do the basic work of selection is the Deputy Attorney General. Each administration works out its own pattern for this purpose. Usually a President chooses Supreme Court Justices on the basis of genuinely independent knowledge of his own. Sometimes, but not often, he may know something personally about the judges for the Circuit Court of Appeals. Rarely will he personally know anything about the district judges he is called upon to appoint. This selection is one to be adjusted between each administration and the dominant voice of the majority political party in the state in which the appointee is to serve. As a practical matter, this means the Senators must be satisfied.

Each administration has the problem of how much of the choice it wishes to defer to a Senator and how much it wishes to retain for itself. Some compromise is necessary. The Senate, by a tradition of senatorial courtesy, will not confirm any district judge who is altogether unsatisfactory to a Senator of the majority party from that state. As White once observed, any Senator determined to block a nomination "can go very far toward that end." In case of an out-and-out conflict, the Senator will win and in this case there may be no appointment. This makes the matter doubly political. Any administration wants to please its supporters where it can, and help them to hold office by in turn helping their supporters. Hence, a Democratic administration is extremely likely to appoint Democratic judges, and not only Democrats, but those whose appointments will aid the party in some way.

Appointments became an immense problem in the first year of the

Kennedy Administration because Congress passed the Omnibus Judges bill, creating seventy new judgeships. This, along with the vacancies left over from the Eisenhower Administration and normal turnover, gave President Kennedy in the neighborhood of one hundred appointments to make during White's period as Deputy Attorney General, more appointments than any previous President has made in an eight-year term. All this was on top of the rest of the normal appointments of any new administration, including choosing staff for ninety-one United States Attorney and United States Marshal offices.

White has given his own description of the process of choosing judges. "We receive recommendations from all sorts of sources; Senators, Congressmen, political organizations in the state, local Bar Associations, State Bar Associations, from individuals and even from the candidates themselves. These names we take and examine.

"We do our own direct checking to some extent in the community and then, from these names, we select one or more which we submit to the Judiciary Committee of the American Bar Association for an informal opinion. When we have that informal opinion, then we do some further checking.

"After this, we then usually select one name and give it to the Judiciary Committee of the American Bar Association for a final opinion and, at the same time, we likewise start an F.B.I. investigation.

"When these two processes are finished and the results are favorable, we normally send a recommendation to the White House that this person be nominated and then the White House either agrees with us or it doesn't; it either sends the name up to the Senate or it doesn't.

"If it sends the name up, the Judiciary Committee of the Senate holds a hearing and considers the matter and then the Senate either confirms the nomination or it doesn't."

A President or a Department of Justice is not obligated to consult the Bar Association at all. The extent to which they do so is a matter of their own choice. Neither the Eisenhower nor the Kennedy

Administrations asked the Bar Association to originate names for consideration; this is for the Senators and for local supporters. But the Eisenhower Administration did give the American Bar Association in effect a veto right, appointing no one whom the Association found unqualified. The Kennedy Administration gave the Association somewhat less authority but it very rarely appointed anyone whom the Association found unqualified.

White's personal processing of appointments was his most time-consuming activity. The American Bar Association Committee, headed by its veteran Chairman, Mr. Bernard Segal of Philadelphia, made a total of five hundred and sixty-four reports during the first year of White's Department of Justice service, an average of two reports for every weekday. Most of these reports were made orally directly to White with the result that he and Mr. Segal were on the phone together at every hour of the day and night. During one period, the President appointed sixty-nine judges in forty-seven days. The discussions were as nonpolitical as they could be; Segal had been National Chairman of the Lawyers for Nixon while White was serving as Chairman of the Citizens for Kennedy. The two became excellent friends.

What of the results? Of the first eighty-five appointments made, the American Bar Committee regarded all but seven as in varying degrees qualified, and seven as not qualified. As White told the Bar Association, the fact that the Association may think that a man is unqualified "does not prove that he is unqualified, and does not prove that he should not be appointed, does not prove he will not make a good judge." The fact that the Association thinks a man is qualified also does not necessarily prove this to be true—although the Association worked diligently to reach its conclusions, it was necessarily dependent upon the quality of its local reports, and the local reports themselves were of uneven reliability.

There were always many factors to be taken into account to which a local Bar association might not be as sensitive as a President needs to be. For example, the President and the Attorney General were committed to a Civil Rights program. Appointments, wherever possible, had to be of judges who were temperamentally willing to enforce these laws as they might be declared by Congress or the Supreme Court. A person willing to do this might not get rave notices from the head of his local Bar association. Moreover a President might on occasion, be compelled to accept a dolt in order to pick up a vitally needed vote on some essential of his legislative program.

The appointment record on the whole was remarkably satisfactory. Since the one hundred appointees will doubtless serve for an average of twenty or so years at least, their combined contribution to the public welfare may well be a greater monument to White and Attorney General Kennedy than anything White does on the Court. There does not appear to have been a single really bad appointment to any of the Courts of Appeal, and no recent administration can equal that record. Of the District Judges, there is an appointee in Oklahoma and another in New York who are not expected to make any great mark in the history of the American law but certainly most are satisfactory and many are excellent.

A major appointment triumph for the administration was the advancement of Judge J. Skelly Wright from the District Court in New Orleans to the Court of Appeals for the District of Columbia. Wright is a prodigious figure, one of the great lower court judges of the country. As a trial judge in Louisiana he consistently led the country for work output, running his courtroom with firm, dexterous, and decisive authority. It was Wright's fate to happen to be the District Judge in Louisiana when a whole series of school and other racial problems occurred there, and in carrying out the decisions of the higher courts he was necessarily compelled to go against the wishes of strong political forces in his own state.

Louisiana is part of that region called the Fifth Circuit whose Court of Appeals covers the southern states of Georgia through Texas.

When a vacancy occurred on the Fifth Circuit Court which could very properly be filled by a judge from Louisiana, Wright was the obvious choice for the advancement. The administration found itself in a terrific difficulty. The Senators from Louisiana could be expected to fight Wright's confirmation, and while the doctrine of senatorial courtesy does not apply rigidly to a Court of Appeals appointment, they might well be effective. On the other hand if Wright were not advanced, the Civil Rights program would take the worst possible blow; for every other federal trial judge in the South would know that if he carried out the decisions of the higher courts, his own career would pay for it.

The position was kept vacant for a long time. Finally a solution was managed, much of it by White's handling. The Court of Appeals for the District of Columbia is not regional in its appointments, and because of the large number of government cases which arise there this Court is important out of all proportion to its geographic area. Senatorial courtesy does not apply to the District; the Louisiana Senators could not effectively block Wright if he were advanced to this Court. The President, on the recommendation of the Department of Justice, moved Wright from Louisiana to the District of Columbia Court of Appeals. It was White who called Wright to propose the promotion. Meanwhile the Fifth Circuit vacancy remained to be filled. The administration gave this appointment to a different state, thus leaving Louisiana with no one.

White went to the Supreme Court in place of Charles Whittaker, who retired. The appointment was a natural; White even came from the same region of the country as Whittaker.

The Senate Judiciary Committee hearing on Justice White was a brief, amiable bull session. And yet the hearing has deep meaning in understanding White's character and personality, not for what did happen, but for what did not happen. White as Deputy Attorney General had enforced Civil Rights legislation vigorously. He had personally taken charge of one colorfully troublesome situation. Yet the Southern Senators on the Committee raised no objection to him whatsoever, and, indeed, endorsed him.

White was aware that he was making what was probably the last appearance of his life before this Committee, with whose members he had worked so constantly. As his parting word he was able to say to the Committee Chairman, Senator Eastland of Mississippi, an arch-leader of the anti-civil rights forces, "Personally, I shall miss you all, and you, Mr. Chairman." White had been able to do his business with Senator Eastland, though they faced each other across a great chasm on a vital issue of the day, without loss of mutual personal regard.

The special feature of White's work on the Court is that in a world made up of and surrounded by professionals, his work is so *very* professional. A piece of legal work may be a delight to the initiate in the same way that a dance student may perceive the difficulties and applaud the accomplishment of the ballerina, or the violinist takes special enjoyment from someone else's concert. The phrase "lawyer's lawyer" does not quite fit; the lawyer's lawyer is the lawyer to whom a lawyer in trouble with a big case takes his own problem. And yet the label is suggestive of White; perhaps the phrase a "lawyer's judge" can be made to fit. If, like the dance student and the violinist, a lawyer may be allowed to enjoy the product of pure professionalism in its most neatly executed fashion, then White is his treat.

Take for example the day of May 13, 1963. White handed down two opinions. The central issue in the first was whether a longshore-man unloading a ship who slipped on some loose beams which spilled on the dock because of defective bagging had a claim against the ship for unseaworthiness. The incident occurred on the pier rather than on the boat, and so the first question was whether the location made any difference. White concluded that it did not; two paragraphs covered the subject. Next was whether the ship could be charged with negligence and, in addition, with unseaworthiness because of the state of the cargo. This latter point had never been clearly considered before, although there was some law on the subject. White neatly laid out whatever was worth knowing before holding the ship liable.

White's second opinion of the same date, on a wholly different subject, dealt with "superseniority" in labor disputes. Superseniority is the term applied to an advantage given to strikebreakers which gives them a disproportionately large seniority at the expense of strikers who may later return to work. In the particular case, the strikebreakers were given a twenty-year seniority bonus. White held this an unfair labor practice.

The two opinions teach a good deal about White:

1. The opinions are tidy, orderly, and complete, with every issue picked up, dusted off, and put down where it belongs. The lazy judge avoids his really hard problems by pretending they are not there. White faces his—the practice he had in the Department of asking his subordinates difficult questions he applied on the Court to himself. He asks himself all the difficult questions.

2. An analyst of opinion writing styles once coined the phrase "legal-massive" for a particular type of opinion which collects and uses all of the legal source materials, particularly previous cases, integrating them directly into the sentences of text. The result is a style which only a lawyer could love, but which satisfies a lawyer very completely. Two of the greatest Justices of this century, Brandeis and Stone, wrote this way. The style has fallen into considerable disuse, really for no very good reason except that styles change. White is the closest of the present nine Justices to the Brandeis-Stone style.

3. While the opinions are turned out with all the professional trappings, they are by no means mechanical. In each of these cases, the Court is necessarily making policy. It was never clearly established before that a ship was responsible for unseaworthiness to a longshoreman who slipped on a pier because of defective cargo packing. Now we know. On the superseniority question, the applicable federal laws do not really deal with the topic at all; this particular gimmick has

developed since the law was passed. The Court, therefore, must in effect forge a new rule of law to cover a new and unanticipated situation. White does not shrink from this policy-making assignment, but he does attempt to do it responsibly. This is particularly evident in the Labor Board case where the pros and cons of a rule are fully set forth.

Occasionally in dissent White is a little more vigorous than perhaps he really intends to be. The cases are hard and differences of opinion are inevitable; and difference is not a hanging matter. If White does occasionally push his argument hard, he means no offense; and hence he is likely to dissent "with all due deference" or "respectfully." Nonetheless, he is still picking up those punts on the dead run and charging with them, and so a White dissent is likely to be a lethal attack. An example of vigor, deep conviction, and yet perfect decorum is his 1964 lone dissent on the legality of Cuba's expropriation of sugar interests.

White's patience and precision with detail makes him a real opponent. The details he picks up are not the persnickity little details of no importance; they are the details which may be small by themselves but which together make up the case. A particularly clear illustration is his dissent on the issue of whether, in a particular case coming up from the State of Washington, the state was obligated to give a person who could not afford it a transcript of the evidence at trial. Without the transcript, his appeal would be worthless, yet a production of these transcripts cost money. The State of Washington therefore set up a system whereby the trial court determined whether the case was worth appealing before the expenditure was made. The majority of the Supreme Court held that the Washington system was inadequate. As the majority concluded, a trial judge would usually think that there was no basis for appeal from his own rulings. Washington would have to devise a system by which a higher court would decide whether there was enough to the case to require the evidence to be reduced to writing.

This is a case in which both the majority and the minority seem right. It is true, as a majority says, that as a general principle, to give control of the appeal to the judge appealed from is bound to result in some real injustices. On the other hand, as Justice White develops in dissent, in this particular case, this particular defendant has nothing to complain about. The defendant raised thirteen separate points as to why his conviction ought to be reversed. White did not spend his time with the general principles involved, but instead went to the thirteen points. Analyzing each of these closely, he showed them to be without merit. It would make no difference what the written record showed; these points could not do the defendant any good, regardless. The dissent illustrates a razor-sharp mind slicing up a case until there is not anything left of it.

White was probably the member of the Kennedy Administration who, outside the Massachusetts appointees, had known President Kennedy longest—twenty-five years at the time of the President's death. This does not mean an intimacy for all those years; the relationship was casual for a long time, but it was there. Richard H. Rovere, in a brilliant and affectionate *New Yorker* memorial after President Kennedy's assassination, attempted to get to the essence of that President's administration. Describing Kennedy "and those who were closest to him—those whom he had freely chosen to associate himself with—" Rovere described them as men of bold aims. Not reformers but pragmatists, men who esteemed facts and disparaged ideologies, not do-gooders or planners but men of large thoughts and large intentions, he said. It is an intuitive rather than a demonstrable judgment, but White represents this core of the Kennedy Administration even more than the other Kennedy appointee, Justice Goldberg, who is less fact-oriented and more philosophically motivated. In this sense, White is a perfect representative of the Kennedy Administration on the high Court.

It is too early to know how White will use the opportunity which his own talents have earned and which John F. Kennedy gave him. Given normal life expectancy, he will serve longer into the future than any of his fellow Justices; he may well be on the Bench for twenty-five years. But it is not too soon to assess how he will do his job. It will be careful, thorough, factual, and, in the best sense of the term, professional.

© Karsh of Ottawa 1964

Chapter Ten

MR. JUSTICE

Arthur Goldberg

JUSTICE GOLDBERG'S approach to the Court and his job on it can be illustrated by fitting together three kinds of decisions he has made.

When the Justice was asked whether he would sit for pictures in this book, his response, like most of the other responses, was cordial and immediate. He thought it was a fine idea, something he was certainly for—if the Chief Justice and Justice Black should also think so. As he saw it, the question of whether Justices should have their pictures taken was a matter of taste. It seemed fine to him. But the older and more experienced members of the Court were the best judges of what was good taste for the Court.

On another occasion, the Justice discussed with an old acquaintance his acceptance of President Kennedy's request that he arbitrate the issues of a then pending national railroad strike. The President had asked him to arbitrate and he had agreed to do so, if both sides desired. The railroads said yes, but the unions declined, and so the matter went to a different solution which did not involve the Justice; but he had agreed to do the job and he explained the factors which had caused him to make up his mind.

It had been an unconventional judgment. Since 1790, the members of the Court have repeatedly faced the problem of whether they should accept any outside duty apart from judging. The heavy weight of tradition and opinion has been in the negative; most Justices have felt that the Court suffers if its members take on anything else. Most feel that 180,000,000 people can afford to reserve nine persons for judging and nothing else. However, for random illustration of exceptions, Justice Bradley did accept the responsibility of deciding who had been legally elected President of the United States in the hard-fought election of 1876; Justice Roberts accepted the task of reviewing just what had happened at Pearl Harbor; Justice Jackson went off to Nuremberg to try the war criminals; and Chief Justice Warren accepted the chairmanship of the commission to investigate the assassination of President Kennedy.

Justice Goldberg was willing to do the railroad arbitration. As he explained to his acquaintance, he followed the views of Judge Parker, a very distinguished lower-court judge who had written that a judge should not be restricted to exclusively Court functions. Goldberg thought Parker's argument persuasive. He would not, he explained, have accepted the duty of mediating the dispute, which is to say that he would not have attempted to bring the two sides together by persuading them or negotiating a compromise, because this he thought was not a suitable job for a judge, though he was willing to decide their case if they wished to have him decide it. "But," he added, "I shall not accept such a request again. Most of the other Justices very clearly think that it is the wrong thing to do."

On the other hand, in his first year and a half on the Court, Justice Goldberg in case after case showed striking independence. He brought to his work a freshness of outlook which directly involved him in making more "new law" than any first year Justice within memory. Rarely has a new broom swept so much dust.

Put the three judgments together, and the result is a free-thinking and original mind, but one under firm control. Picture-taking is, of course, of little or no consequence; the Justice will defer to his elders. Arbitrating a labor dispute is of substantial consequence; it involves the whole Court. Goldberg's arbitration affects others, perhaps adding to their work load, perhaps reducing his own efficiency just a little. It is not his present primary responsibility. Therefore again, once he clearly knows how his fellow judges feel, he will defer to them.

But the business of deciding how to vote and how to express himself on the cases before the Supreme Court is his primary duty. In this he can defer to no one, for the ultimate responsibility of judgment is his alone and this is the precise job which has been given him. That job he will perform with the unlimited freshness of approach of a genuinely enterprising mind.

In the late nineteenth century the American novelist Horatio Alger wrote a series of novels on boys of poor beginnings rising to greatness, some of the most famous being *Ragged Dick, Luck and Pluck* and *Tattered Tom.* If Alger had lived another sixty years, he doubtless would have turned out a work on "Able Arthur," for Goldberg fits the format; he would have been the first Alger hero with a Jewish name. The room at the Supreme Court in which Justice Goldberg's picture was taken for this volume happens to contain the portrait of John Jay, the first Chief Justice of the United States, appointed by George Washington in 1789. No one whose eye travels from the portrait of the first Justice to the flesh-and-blood reality of the most recent can fail to be reminded of the extraordinary range of American opportunity; for the gap in backgrounds between the patrician Jay and Goldberg, the immigrant's son, is as great as the span of time which separates them.

Goldberg's father came out of the Ukraine in Russia by way of Siberia and Manchuria, landing in San Francisco in 1894. His mother, Rebecca Perlstein, came from Russia two years later. By the time Arthur was born on August 8, 1908, his father had moved to Texas and then Illinois, and was an established but by no means prosperous fruit peddler in Chicago. Goldberg as a youngster rode with his father behind a blind horse and brought home the leftover fruit to share with the other kids in the thoroughly rough slum neighborhood. While Goldberg was eventually to make the most important political alliance of his life with the man who became the first Irish President of the United States, the pre-World War I relations of the Irish and Jewish population of Chicago were by no means so amiable. Goldberg recalls brick fights between Jewish and Irish youngsters when he was still too young to do more than carry the bricks for someone else to throw.

As a high school boy and as a student both at Crane Junior College in Chicago and at Northwestern Law School, from which he got law degrees in 1929 and 1930, Goldberg worked his way. In high school he was a delivery boy for a shoe factory. Later he was on the night shift at the post office, and spent summers working as a laborer in construction gangs. His upbringing was in the style of good Russian Orthodox Jewry. His grandfather, who also immigrated to Chicago, was a rabbi, and his father was president of their small synagogue. Goldberg recalls that as his father wandered about America before settling in Chicago, he found some of the synagogues not very friendly to travelers. When Goldberg, Senior, himself became head of a synagogue, he saw to it that two pews were at all times reserved for strangers.

Goldberg not only worked his way through Northwestern Law School, but graduated first in his class. He graduated just in time to experience the worst depression in the history of the United States. His first opportunity to vote in a presidential election came in 1932, and Franklin D. Roosevelt was very clearly the man for him. FDR gave him a permanent bent in the direction of a liberal democracy.

For the first years of Goldberg's practice, he was not involved in labor matters, and if the commercial law practice of those years had been a little better he might have gone on to become a corporate lawyer; but times were hard and the Wagner Labor Relations Act of 1935 launched a labor boom in the late 1930's which for a time made the practice of labor law the most exciting brand of law in the United States. The labor law of more recent years has frequently tended to be routine stuff—problems of contract negotiations and drafting or arbitration are not much different from those of any other form of business enterprise. But in the late 1930's, the CIO was founded and the greatest organizational drive in the history of the United States

168

began, with plenty for a young lawyer to do who had no more profitable way to spend his time. Goldberg was drawn to the organization of the steel mills in the Chicago area, and while there were times when the revenues were hardly enough to let him and the organizer split a beer and a sandwich, more stable times were ahead. In the same period he also represented the newspaper guild and was deeply involved in a colorful strike in Chicago.

The sudden labor-union boom gave Communists an opportunity to infiltrate some of the expanding labor organizations, and Goldberg thus had a chance to see them at work. He found the Communists a destructive force in any organization, and he was always completely independent of them. During the same period, he withdrew from the National Lawyers Guild because he felt that it was subject to Communist infiltration.

By the beginning of World War II, Goldberg had developed a considerable labor practice, particularly for the steelworkers. During the war he went into the Office of Strategic Services with a most exceptional cloak-and-dagger assignment. Serving first as a captain and later as a major in the army, he was head of the labor division for OSS. Several times he went to Europe and North Africa to organize trade unions wherever he could find them to undertake espionage work in the Allied cause. He secured the help not only of resistance workers in France and Holland but also some in Italy, Germany, and the Middle East who fed back vital information for the Allied bombing program.

After the war, Goldberg's practice moved into high gear and for the late 1940's and throughout the 1950's, he was the most prominent labor lawyer in America. In 1948, CIO president Philip Murray concluded that the time had come to get the Reds out of the CIO, and to aid in this, appointed Goldberg as General Counsel both for the CIO and for the steelworkers. Goldberg also wanted individual Communist leaders or any Communist unions out, and at the same time he wanted fair procedures for determining the facts. But while Goldberg

169

was chief counsel for the unions, he was never willing to risk his independence altogether, and he kept his law office open and functioning rather than going directly onto a union payroll.

Goldberg's objection to the Communists and his maintenance of his own personal independence are keys to the understanding of his conception of the labor movement and of his own role in connection with it. The whole idea of a proletarian revolution as a result of which unions should rule the country is to him foolishness; he did not even wish to have them rule one American, Arthur Goldberg, much less the rest of his fellow citizens. His policy was the exact opposite of the destruction of capitalism; his goal was to increase labor's stake in it. His was the approach of increased fringe benefits, of welfare programs for the sick, and retirement programs for the aged. He was one of the designers of the system of keying labor's return to the productivity and profit of the industry in which the employee worked. One of his primary cases as a union lawyer was the establishment of the principle that pensions were a legitimate object of collective bargaining.

The Goldberg stock in trade became an amalgam of energy and reasonableness, two qualities which very often do not go together. The duo served his clients well, both at the bargaining table, where, when impasse was reached, he searched for new solutions, and within the unions themselves.

The largest achievement with which Goldberg is associated was the merger of the American Federation of Labor and the Congress of Industrial Organizations. These two bodies had gone their separate ways from 1935 to 1955, occasionally to the detriment of the country. As counsel for the CIO, Goldberg pushed a consolidation, and had a very substantial hand in achieving it. The merger was difficult because it meant sacrifices of personal ambition and status for many of the men involved. The result was a kind of alliance which has at least the form and some of the substance of unity. Goldberg was, oddly enough, one of the first victims of his own accomplishment—someone else was chosen to be chief counsel for the consolidated organization with Goldberg remaining as chief legal adviser to the segments he had previously represented.

Nonetheless, from this point on, Goldberg had great influence on both sides of the organization. His greatest post-merger responsibility was in the expulsion of corrupt unions from the organization. He prepared the ethical practices code under which the Teamsters, the Bakery and Confectionery Workers' unions, and others were dropped from the AFL–CIO. During this period, which came in the late 1950's, corruption and racketeering were being investigated by the Committee of Senator McClellan, whose chief counsel was Robert Kennedy. Goldberg supported Senator Kennedy's labor reform measure of 1958, and won support for it from organized labor, hardly an easy assignment.

In the thirty years of his practice from 1930 to his entry into the Kennedy Cabinet after the 1960 election, Goldberg tried many cases. He remembers vividly one of the first, a 1930 matter in the Supreme Court of Illinois in which he served as unpaid, appointed counsel. The issue was whether juries could be given the power to decide questions of law as well as of fact, and Goldberg, upholding the jury power, lost. He also handled a leading case in the history of labor arbitration. Another leading labor case was the foundation for what is known as the pre-emption doctrine, the rule that state courts and agencies must largely leave labor disputes affecting interstate commerce to the National Labor Relations Board.

Goldberg's two biggest cases in the Supreme Court both arose from steel strikes. The first involved an order by President Truman, issued only a few hours before a strike was to begin, directing his Secretary of Commerce to take possession of and operate most of the steel mills of the country. If any act of Congress gave the President power to make such a seizure, it was not used; rather, the President justified the seizure on the basis of his inherent powers. Goldberg for the steel unions argued the case on the Government side, and in a company of great lawyers pro and con, was regarded as having distinguished himself though only three Justices agreed with him.

The second great steel case arose from the steel strike of 1959, which stopped almost all of the country's steel production for very nearly four months. The Taft-Hartley Act permits the Government to obtain a court order requiring the suspension of a strike for an eighty-day cooling-off period if the strike affects an entire industry and if it "will imperil the national health or safety."

Acting under the statute, the Government sought an injunction against the steelworkers to stop this strike. Goldberg for the steelworkers argued that whatever else the strike had done, it imperiled neither the national health nor the national safety. The government argued that "national health" included the economic as well as the physical health of the country, while Goldberg argued that this term meant only actual physical welfare. He contended that a small, partial reopening was all that was required for national defense purposes. The Court, Justice Douglas dissenting, put the health issue aside and found that the strike did endanger the national safety, in the sense of the national defense, referring to missiles, space projects, nuclear submarines, and shipbuilding. While the injunction was in effect, Vice President Richard Nixon and Secretary of Labor Mitchell aided in negotiating a settlement which Goldberg regards as a major victory.

Early in 1960, Goldberg and a number of other labor leaders concluded to support John F. Kennedy for the Presidential nomination of the Democratic Party. The judgment as between Kennedy and Lyndon Johnson was not an easy or casual one for Goldberg because he liked and admired Johnson, too. He felt that as a matter of ability the two men were probably about equal and that, if anything, there might be a slight edge in executive experience for Johnson. However, he liked Kennedy's style and he believed that he could be nominated and elected. He worked hard for that result.

After the election, there was some doubt as to the post Goldberg would fill in the new administration. Some thought he might become Attorney General or perhaps Solicitor General, that officer of the Department of Justice responsible for the Government's cases in the Supreme Court. He himself had some preference for a more strictly legal post than that which he finally accepted. When the President spoke to him about becoming Secretary of Labor, Goldberg questioned whether it was appropriate for a labor representative to take the office, and suggested that there should be someone more non-partisan in that Cabinet seat. But the President made his choice, and Goldberg undertook his job.

He began with a bang and quickly became one of the most active and most successful members of the Kennedy Administration. The very day he took office, he whizzed up to New York to settle a harbor workers' strike, and from then on his program was one of go, go, go.

Goldberg wrought a revolution in the Labor Department by doing exactly what the chief adviser of the President of the United States on labor relations is supposed to do. The Labor Department had for many years been not the policy-making heart of the administration on all labor matters but simply a collection of minor bureaus. President Eisenhower's Secretary James Mitchell brought it to life but there was still a tremendous amount to be done. Goldberg accepted the office with the express understanding with the President that this was to be a key Department of the administration and that all of the power and responsibility which had dribbled away or lain unexercised over the years Goldberg would assume.

Labor disputes were the first area of Secretarial direction. As Goldberg once said, "You know me—I'm an activist," and in labor disputes he certainly was. Some questioned whether Goldberg was getting into more labor disputes than a Secretary should. Very regularly his intervention was helpful, as for example in the General Motors strike, in the Maritime Union strike, and in the airlines strike. However, he did so much more than his predecessors that there was some risk of overcentralizing the office. If everyone thought that his strike was going to be settled by a Cabinet member, settlements might be delayed while the parties waited for him. Not even Superman—or Super-Secretary—could settle any very large portion of the labor disputes in the United States.

Goldberg understood these dangers and did not believe that he was intervening too often. He went into any dispute which because of its national nature would probably end up on the President's desk; if he could head these off, he was helping the economy and saving the President's time. He usually turned down the purely local disputes, leaving their disposition to less spectacular processes.

To this there were only two exceptions. One was a matter in Cleveland. While giving a speech there, so many people asked him to lend a hand with a local dispute that he finally agreed to see the parties for a few minutes as a courtesy to his hosts. He did, made a suggestion, and its acceptance did dispose of that particular strike.

The other, and more spectacular, incident was the Metropolitan Opera dispute in 1961. This was not national in terms of the economy, but it was national in the sense of a nation-wide interest in the opera. It appeared that an entire opera season might be washed out. The President called his Secretary and told him that Mrs. Kennedy had asked him to do something. The President stressed that the cultural reputation of the United States was seriously at stake if the major American opera company should shut down. As he put it to Goldberg, the world thinks America is too materialistic anyway; a musical collapse would accentuate this impression. The President expressly did not tell Goldberg to go into the dispute; it was never the President's practice to give his Secretary orders, and the final judgment was left to Goldberg.

Goldberg thought it over and concluded to go in. Not only was he persuaded by the argument, but he is an opera fan. His intervention did result in a disposition of the dispute and the production of a Metropolitan season.

In part, Goldberg's interventions were because he is against strikes on the merits. In a world of rising Soviet power and increasing European competition, he believes that the sheer waste of protracted strikes is a luxury the country cannot afford. He would completely maintain free collective bargaining including the right to strike, but he also believes that the Government should take the lead to try to avoid these problems. Some of his old labor associates and some business executives took a sharply different view; but Goldberg as a representative of the public saw no excuse for letting private wars cripple the economy when this was avoidable.

Goldberg had several other major functions for the administration. One was public relations. He made more speeches throughout the country than any other two or three Cabinet members. He was also the administration's policy man on labor relations and on all matters of direct concern both to the employed and the unemployed. He had to devise legislation to carry out these policy programs and to see the legislation through Congress.

He saw the need of creating new jobs and new job training as a result of the increase in automation. He went up to Congress so often that one portion of the lobby came to be called the "Goldberg Room." The results were spectacular. Almost every single significant Congressional success of the Kennedy Administration was on his bills. He secured an extension of the temporary unemployment compensation period of coverage. He saw through the amendments to the Fair Labor Standards Act raising the minimum wage to $1.25 an hour and extending the Act to some three and one-half million new people. He obtained legislation for retraining jobless workers, particularly those losing their positions because of automation, and his Department began a hundred retraining projects for thousands of employees. He instituted a major new program for training unemployed young people. On a vote by a large number of Senators and Representatives, only Secretary McNamara was thought to have done a better job than he in the Kennedy Cabinet.

In August of 1962, Justice Frankfurter sent his retirement letter to the President. The President immediately, before public announcement was made, called Goldberg over to the White House. Goldberg had been about to see the President on a wholly different problem to report that a strike in Chicago required him to go there rather than on a Presidential mission to Trinidad. Someone had to catch a five-o'clock plane to Trinidad in his place, and he wanted to suggest Judge William Hastie of the United States Court of Appeals at Philadelphia. Hence, when the President opened the conversation Goldberg said cheerfully, "Mr. President, I have worse troubles than you do; would you mind taking up my problem first?"

The President smiled and agreed, accepted the Hastie suggestion, and called him instantly. That matter disposed of, the President explained that the retirement of Justice Frankfurter would shortly be announced and told Goldberg that the Secretary was his choice for the vacancy.

The suggestion did not take Goldberg altogether by surprise, although there had been no previous direct discussion of the matter between the two. The President knew of Goldberg's interest in strictly legal work. When Justice White had been appointed, the President had called Goldberg before the announcement to tell him of the appointment, a somewhat exceptional courtesy. Goldberg replied to the President that while he would like the seat very much, the administration was still so new that he ought to stay on his job in the Labor Department until a later time. He suggested that perhaps the President could give him the chance later, although he would not in any sense be obligated to do so. The President replied that he felt to the contrary, that Goldberg on the Court would long outlast the Kennedy Administration and that he felt that the Secretary's temporary utility to the President should be put aside. He asked Goldberg to suggest his own successor, and Goldberg recommended his Undersecretary, Willard Wirtz. The last word between the two was Goldberg's suggestion that the President give the matter additional thought.

Goldberg thereupon left for Chicago. When he arrived he discovered that the President could not have given it very much additional thought because the appointment was announced at once. President Kennedy's letter of appointment was exceptionally affectionate. He said:

You have been a wise and invaluable member of the innermost councils of this administration, and your voice, counsel and tireless efforts will be sorely missed. But you shall bring distinction to our highest court many years after this administration is gone; and I do not feel that I can deny our country and Constitution these benefits of your talents and service.

Goldberg returned for a confirmation by the Senate which was as much an accolade as is any approval by that body for a high post. Labor was of course pleased. But the endorsements came also from the Republicans. Senate Majority Leader Everett Dirksen said that the Secretary "measures up to every standard required for a place on the Supreme Court." Senator Barry Goldwater, as ranking Republican member of the Senate Labor Committee, was equally enthusiastic.

There was a little carping, but surprisingly little. David Lawrence thought that the appointment was purely political. There were a few other critics. But the favorable outpouring was astounding. The endorsement of the Illinois State Bar Association came from its President, a Republican, who represented management in labor disputes, and who thought Goldberg exceptionally well qualified. It was to be expected that his legal associates and his former clients would support him, but so did the Aluminum Company of America and other employers. The American Merchant Marine Institute, representative of the employers in that industry, wrote that when Goldberg had been appointed Secretary of Labor "the entire management segment of our industry approved of the appointment . . . his reputation for honesty, fairness and objectivity was well known throughout the shipping industry." As the representative said, this attitude is "quite remarkable when you consider Mr. Goldberg's long career within the ranks of labor."

Most touching of all were the words from the representatives of

Goldberg's long-time adversary, the steel industry. From Jones & Laughlin Steel Corporation: "Friendly . . . very great admiration for him . . . keen and well educated mind . . . absolute integrity . . . outstanding lawyer." From United States Steel: "Will make an excellent judge, and will indeed bring credit to the office to which he has been nominated." From Republic Steel, "Highest degree of professional ability and character . . . integrity and vigor . . . invaluable practical experience."

The interrogation of Goldberg by the Senate Judiciary Committee was friendly. He reviewed his own background, was asked a few questions about whether Justices needed prior judicial experience (he thought not), and talked a little legal philosophy with Senator Ervin of North Carolina. He commented briefly on when a Justice might feel free to overrule an earlier opinion and when he must follow it, saying innocuously enough that there should be an overruling only when the Justice had "the profound conviction that there is such a fundamental error that it must be redressed."

Senator Wiley, the ranking Republican on the Committee, told Goldberg that he had received some letters suggesting that Goldberg was a Communist, and asking the Secretary to comment. Wiley's question was a friendly one; the Senator assured the Secretary that anyone "not completely prejudiced" would certainly realize that Goldberg had "never been a Communist and [was] not sympathetic toward their philosophy." Goldberg handed the Senator a chapter from his book, *The A.F. of L.-C.I.O.; Labor United,* which he asked to be included in the hearings. The chapter fully illustrates Goldberg's view that Communism is a "perversion of what people have a right to expect from government and from life."

A Congressional Committee can investigate the record of a nominee, but its crystal ball is no better than anyone else's for guessing what the nominee will do in the future. The one question in some minds was whether Goldberg as a Justice would be fair to both management and labor or whether his long labor association would prejudice him in the union direction. His administration as Secretary had so largely set minds at rest that this was not much of an issue. However, Senator McClellan gave Goldberg an opportunity to say on this:

One of the high obligations of a Justice of the Supreme Court is to guard against—perhaps the highest—is to guard against putting into his opinion his own private predilections. And I would hope that all the human feelings that a man has, that if the Senate confirms my appointment, that I will be able to see to it that when I participate in the Court's opinions, that I will be able to prevent my own views as a private citizen, my own predilections, my own prejudices—I have them, because I am a human being—from being exalted into legal principle.

Goldberg was swiftly confirmed and took his seat in the beginning of the 1962 term of the Supreme Court. Less than two months later, the Court handed down its first formal opinions of the year and Goldberg's first opinion was the first presented. It was an antitrust case having to do with block booking in the movie industry, and with it Goldberg was off on his new career.

The law is usually reasonable. The Mr. Bumble of Dickens says, "If the law supposes that, the law is a ass, a idiot." Sometimes the law is "a ass, a idiot," but happily not often. More often than not—indeed, most of the time—the law is simply an elaborate rigamarole for doing what common sense dictates.

To this there is at least one exception. For some reason, in dealing with aliens, immigrants who have been settled here sometimes for decades, the law loses all reason and frequently becomes wildly arbitrary. As a carryover, in dealing with the citizenship of native-born American citizens, the law has frequently been just as arbitrary.

Take, for example, the problem of re-entry. In the 1930's the Supreme Court held that an alien who had been here for twenty-four years and who left to make a brief visit to Cuba should be treated upon his return as if he had never come at all. If a complete stranger would have been ineligible to enter for the first time, then the traveler also was barred and could not return to his family, his home, his business and his life in our land. The situations—the one an immigrant coming for the first time and the other the immigrant who spends a weekend just over the border—are so utterly different that the law ought to be able to make a distinction between them; but for a long time it could not.

In the 1940's the courts began to chip away a little at this harsh doctrine. One court held that where an alien took a train from Chicago to New York which happened to run through a little bit of Canada while he was sound asleep, he should not be regarded as a stranger on his re-entry; and a little later the Supreme Court held that when an alien was serving the American Merchant Marine during World War II and his boat was torpedoed, resulting in his being put ashore on some alien soil briefly until he could get transportation home, he was not to be regarded as if he were coming for the first time.

In 1963 this old problem was back again. An alien who had been in this country for four years spent a couple of hours on a brief afternoon excursion into Mexico. This time Justice Goldberg wrote the decision. He declared that the laws could not be "woodenly construed" and that an insignificant, casual trip should not be allowed to become a trap. Calling for a "more civilized application of our immigration laws," he held that "an innocent, casual and brief excursion by a resident alien outside this country's borders" is not to be regarded as putting the alien in the same position as if he had never been here at all. In a 1964 dissent he vainly sought to push the principle of this case a little farther, involving the "humane purposes" of the applicable law when the Government sought to deport, because of a previous departure, an alien who had served a couple of months on an Allied merchant ship during World War II, and under Government pressure at that. If, by some stupendous change of course, the law ever comes to the conclusion that aliens are entitled to the minimum decencies of common humanity, Goldberg will probably lead the way.

Goldberg applied this same common-sense approach to the infinitely more important problem of the right of an American citizen to retain his citizenship. It is the law under the Constitution that no person charged with even the most minor offense shall be punished without due process of law. If someone is charged with shoplifting from a neighborhood shore, he is entitled to a charge, to a lawyer to defend him, and to a chance to examine the witnesses against him, to a jury trial; else he cannot be convicted. Yet if an American citizen is abroad, under one Act of Congress a government agency has been given the power to take his citizenship away from him without giving him any hearing, any trial, any chance to examine witnesses, any lawyer in his own defense, or any jury trial. A man may be turned into a stateless wanderer with no home of his own, no government to protect him, the victim of any tyranny which may exist on this broad globe without any day in court whatsoever. This remarkable result has been reached on the theory that fining a man $500 or putting him in jail for thirty days is "punishment"; but taking away his citizenship is not "punishment," and therefore the man has no rights whatsoever.

In 1963, Justice Goldberg for the Court handed down an opinion declaring this Act of Congress unconstitutional. In what may well be one of the finest as well as one of the most elaborate opinions he will ever write on the Court, the Justice put aside the "no punishment" theory. The son of immigrants himself, Goldberg is in a position to know, as he said, that this was "an issue of the utmost import. Deprivation of citizenship—particularly American citizenship, which is 'one of the most valuable rights in the world today,' has grave practical consequences." A person with no citizenship is said to be "stateless" and, as the Justice said, "the stateless person may end up shunted from nation to nation, there being no one obligated or willing to receive him, or . . . receive the dubious sanctuary of a Communist regime lacking the essential liberties precious to American citizenship."

The opinion illustrates Goldberg's realism and practicality. The absentees were said to be draft evaders. Goldberg fully endorsed stern and strict punishment for anyone who does evade the draft. But, as he pointed out, these persons may have been absent for some wholly innocent reason—perhaps for illness, perhaps inability to come back. They are entitled to a fair trial to determine the reason for their absence.

But, it was suggested, these persons might never return and so might never be punished. Then, said Goldberg, what is the difference? So long as they were gone, the United States need not be much bothered with them; the question of how much protection they get abroad is for the State Department to decide. And, should they ever return, they can face the music—not as the result of some order by a bureaucrat who has never seen them and on the basis of reports coming from Heaven knows where, but on the basis of clear evidence in open court, in the American way.

Goldberg wrote on one more alien case in 1963. A Mexican had come to this country in 1920 as a ten-year-old boy. He had raised and supported a family in this country, all of whom are American citizens. In 1949 and 1950 he had paid some dues to and attended some meetings of a club of the Communist Party.

The issue was whether he could be deported. Goldberg recognized that many uneducated persons in minority groups may know nothing of the international significance of Communism and may think that it is simply another local movement to remedy hardships, discrimination, or poverty in the United States. The clear import of the Goldberg opinion is that if a man is to be put out of the United States after forty-three years of residence, smashing a family for some association he is supposed to have had many years before, there must be very clear evidence of wrongdoing.

These Goldberg opinions make a pattern of humanity and originality; each moves the law a step further than it was before. But they by no means show a pattern of sentimentality as though Goldberg were trying only to find the kindly thing to do and then do it. Goldberg is by no means a sentimentalist; for example, in one of the injured railroad worker cases he took a much narrower view of the duties of the railroads than almost all of his associates because he felt that the law was not with the injured worker. The common thread of the three alien cases is the reasonableness of the result. When an alien is out of the country for two hours after several years of residence here, it is unreasonable to put him in the same category as a person who has never been here at all. Taking away American citizenship is one of the extremest possible forms of punishment and should be recognized as such. Literature has no trouble recognizing the awful plight of "The Man Without a Country," and the law should have no more. There ought to be a substantial proof of guilt before a person is deported who has been in this country for more than forty years. No one will ever fairly level Bumble's criticism at Goldberg.

Goldberg's method of doing his work must be the most remarkable the Court has ever seen. He dictates the first draft of his opinions, not to a dictating machine or to a secretary, but directly to his law clerk. He thinks the draft through, laying it out slowly enough that the clerk, by a mixture of writing and quick notes, can put down what he says. He prefers the clerk to a secretary because the clerk can understand the substance of what he is doing. If he wishes to pass over something lightly, with a simple allusion, he can do so, because the clerk will understand cryptic legal references. If he wishes to illustrate with something so obvious that there are clearly case authorities to support him, he can say, "Put in citations," or "Refer to a case or two by brief reference," and the clerk, with a little give and take in the conversation, can know what he has in mind. Goldberg worked this way when he was practicing law, and he likes it.

The clerk, who is wholly untrained in shorthand, thereupon carries out of the room what must be a frightful mess of notes and converts it into a draft which he sends back to the Justice. The Justice then works over the draft, scrawling it up entirely, going over each word, writing notes in the margin for additions or deletions, putting in interlineations, and generally rehashing it. In a typical instance, no line may be untouched when the Justice finishes this revise. The clerk himself inserts his own suggestions on the same draft, to be included or scratched out as the Justice prefers.

This is then retyped and the process begins anew, though presumably with fewer alterations as drafts advance. The minimum number of drafts is usually four, and in serious cases the opinion may go through ten before it is ready to be circulated to the other Justices for their comments.

It is too early in Goldberg's career to know whether his opinions will have a clearly definable style so that an expert, reading unidentified paragraphs, would know fairly readily that he had written them. His opinions are comparatively brief, not much given to scholarly elaboration, and, without exception, never exhibitions of fancy phraseology. A man of his quick facility could be tempted into butterfly-chasing, or fairly aimless opinions, elaborating in some way on the opinions of the Court. Such exercises, while sometimes instructive, usually only consume energy which would more usefully be put elsewhere. One of the very rare instances of a Goldberg concurrence "by way of comment on the dissenting opinion of my brother Stewart" is happily just that—a very rare instance. A businesslike fellow, Justice Goldberg—direct, concise, hard-hitting, and imaginative.

Goldberg thoroughly enjoys being Jewish. Although he follows the reformed Jewish faith, he saw to it that his son had training of a more conservative Jewish variety. He has been active in large numbers of Jewish organizations and brought a rabbi with him for the Senate hearings on his own confirmation. He enjoys Jewish food, and takes pleasure in introducing friends to it. He has escaped the twin hazards of timidity and aggressiveness to reach a plateau, a kind of joyous Jewishness, a serene sense of security.

What Jacob Potofsky, the President of the Amalgamated Clothing Workers, said when Goldberg was appointed to the Court, was this:

> Our membership consists of many kinds of Americans: people of every race and people from Southern states like Georgia and Mississippi and Northern states like Illinois and New York; people whose families have lived in this nation for generations and people new or relatively new to our American shores. In serving these people, in seeking to achieve a better life for themselves and their families, the Amalgamated Clothing Workers have benefited greatly from the philosophy of Arthur Goldberg.

> Now the Secretary represents everybody; and the benefit of the philosophy should be felt by all Americans.

© Karsh of Ottawa 1964

References

This section contains references that may be useful to others in checking sources of quotes or specific decisions.

CHAPTER ONE   The Supreme Court

The document volume referred to as illustrating the different prominence of Supreme Court opinions at various points in American history is Henry Steele Commager's *Documents of American History* (New York, Appleton-Century-Crofts, 6th edition, 1958). My article "Court and Constitution: The Passive Period" appeared in the April, 1951, *Vanderbilt Law Review,* p. 400. The quotations from the attacks on Chief Justice Marshall in 1821 come from Charles Warren, *The Supreme Court in United States History* (Boston, Little, Brown, 1960), Vol. 1, pp. 555–556. The statistical analysis of the work of the Court is collected each year in the *Report of the Administrator of the United States Courts,* and among other places I have summarized such information in *Marble Palace,* Chapter I (New York, Alfred A. Knopf, 1958). The last paragraph of this chapter I liked well enough to take bodily from my article "The Historic Role of the Supreme Court" in the Fall, 1959, *Kentucky Law Journal* (48 *Ky. L. J.* pp. 26, 46–47).

CHAPTER TWO   Chief Justice Earl Warren

The description of Warren's original method of admitting lawyers to the Bar is taken from my article in *The New York Times* magazine section, "Affirmative Opinion on Justice Warren," October 3, 1954, p. 17. The contemporary observation is my own, but the spontaneous expression of surprise at Warren's capacity to treat all these individuals in a manner that would make each feel welcome is by Mrs. Karsh on the occasion of her first visit to the Court. The description of Warren at a meeting of the American Law Institute is taken from the 1963 meeting at the Mayflower Hotel in Washington.

The quotations from various of Warren's speeches are taken from Henry M. Christman, editor, *The Public Papers of Chief Justice Earl Warren* (New York, Simon & Schuster, 1959). The quotation on trust comes from page 4, that on social objectives from page 12, that on the Bill of Rights from page 7, and on religious tolerance from page 16. The letter to the Chinese is quoted in the 1954 *New York Times* article cited above, and I must confess that I no longer know where I got it at that time.

The quotation from Adlai Stevenson appears in *Adlai Stevenson— Major Campaign Speeches,* p. 112 (New York, Random House, Inc.). The reference to Secretary Dulles as a possible Chief Justice is made in Robert J. Donovan, *Eisenhower—The Inside Story,* pp. 161–162 (New York, Harper & Brothers, 1956). The basic school-segregation case was *Brown v. Board of Education of Topeka,* 347 U.S. 483, 74 Sup. Ct. 686, 98 L. Ed. 873 (1954). The leading case on segregation and landholding is *Shelley v. Kraemer,* 334 U.S. 1, 68 Sup. Ct. 836, 92 L. Ed. 1161 (1948), and the case on segregation and higher education is *Sweatt v. Painter,* 339 U.S. 629, 70 Sup. Ct. 848, 94 L. Ed. 1114 (1950). There are innumerable accounts of the progress of desegregation, one of them being Allan P. Sindler, editor, *Change in the Contemporary South* (Durham, N.C., Duke University Press, 1963), including a chapter of my own, "Legal Developments and Race Relations, 1945–1962." The decision that the unconstitutionality of segregation was beyond discussion, is *Bailey v. Patterson,* 369 U.S. 31, 82 Sup. Ct. 549, 7 L. Ed. 2d 512 (1962). The decision on legislative investigations is *Watkins v. United States,* 354 U.S. 178, 77 Sup. Ct. 1173, 1 L. Ed. 2d 1273 (1957).

The electronic-recording case quoted is *Lopez v. United States,* 373 U.S. 427, 83 Sup. Ct. 1381, 10 L. Ed. 2d 462 (1963). The 1963 decision relating to the House Committee on Un-American Activities, is *Yellin v. United States,* 374 U.S. 109, 83 Sup. Ct. 1828, 10 L. Ed.

2d 778 (1963). The quotation on military justice and procedure comes from a lecture given at New York University on February 1, 1962, titled "The Bill of Rights and the Military." The memorial address for President Kennedy is contained in the *Congressional Record* for November 25, 1963, at 1096, *Cong. Rec.* 21592, 88th Cong., 1st Sess.

CHAPTER THREE   Mr. Justice Hugo L. Black

This chapter draws freely on two of my own writings on Black, one, *Mr. Justice Black, The Man and His Opinions* (New York, Alfred A. Knopf, 1949), and the other, "Mr. Justice Black: A Biographical Appreciation," 65 *Yale L. J.* 454 (1956), on which I have drawn particularly heavily. *Betts* v. *Brady* is reported at 316 U.S. 455, 62 Sup. Ct. 1252, 86 L. Ed. 1595 (1942). This and many other subjects are comprehensively discussed by Professor Charles A. Reich in *Mr. Justice Black,* 76 *Harv. L. Rev.* 673 (1963). The overruling decision is *Gideon* v. *Wainwright,* 372 U.S. 335, 83 Sup. Ct. 792, 9 L. Ed. 2d 799 (1963). The 1964 equal-representation case is *Wesberry* v. *Sanders,* 84 Sup. Ct. 526, 11 L. Ed. 2d 481 (1964). For identification of other decisions in the eight-point list of important matters in the text, see the article of Professor Reich, *supra.*

The quotation from Charles Beard is from the introduction to my *Mr. Justice Black* book, pp. xii-xiv. The quotation on the Seventh Amendment comes from *Galloway* v. *United States,* 319 U.S. 372, 63 Sup. Ct. 1077, 87 L. Ed. 1458 (1943). The Bethlehem Steel case referred to is the *United States* v. *Bethlehem Steel Corp.,* 315 U.S. 289, 62 Sup. Ct. 581, 86 L. Ed. 855 (1942), and the steel-seizure case is *Youngstown Sheet & Tube Co.* v. *Sawyer,* 343 U.S. 579, 72 Sup. Ct. 863, 96 L. Ed. 1153 (1952). The quotation on the absolute nature of the right of free speech comes from a commencement address given by Justice Black at Swarthmore College on June 6, 1955. The case developing the view expressed in the Swarthmore lecture is *Baren-*

blatt v. *United States,* 360 U.S. 109, 79 Sup. Ct. 1081, 3 L. Ed. 2d 1115 (1959). The New York Regents prayer case is *Engel* v. *Vitale,* 370 U.S. 421, 82 Sup. Ct. 1261, 8 L. Ed. 2d 601 (1962).

The reference to my own 1956 piece is that in *Yale L. J.,* cited above. The due-process decision is *Ferguson* v. *Skrupa,* 372 U.S. 726, 83 Sup. Ct. 1028, 10 L. Ed. 2d 93 (1963). The airline discrimination case is *Colorado Anti-Discrim. Com'n.* v. *Continental Air L.,* 372 U.S. 714, 83 Sup. Ct. 1022, 10 L. Ed. 2d 84 (1963). *Chambers* v. *Florida* appears at 309 U.S. 227, 60 Sup. Ct. 472, 84 L. Ed. 716 (1940).

CHAPTER FOUR　　Mr. Justice William O. Douglas

The citation to *Dennis* v. *United States* is 341 U.S. 494, 71 Sup. Ct. 857, 95 L. Ed. 1137 (1951). The Douglas opinion follows that of Justice Brandeis in *Whitney* v. *California,* 274 U.S. 357, 47 Sup. Ct. 641, 7 L. Ed. 1095 (1927). The 1945 treason case is *Cramer* v. *United States,* 325 U.S. 1, 65 Sup. Ct. 918, 89 L. Ed. 1441 (1945).

For a reflection of the view early in his SEC experience that Douglas was antibusiness, see *The New York Times,* August 10, 1937, p. 25; but for the "conciliatory" view, see *The New York Times,* November 23, 1938, p. 22. The quotation from Arthur Krock at the time of the Douglas appointment appears in *The New York Times,* March 21, 1939, p. 22. The references to the hearing on the Douglas appointment come from a typescript of the Douglas hearings, March 24, 1939, which was seen by me in that year in the files of the United States Senate Judiciary Committee, but the location of which has not been checked since.

The paragraphs following that synthesize the Douglas opinions are taken from my own review of the book of Professor Vern Countryman, *William O. Douglas of the Supreme Court* (New York, Doubleday & Company, 1959), the review appearing at 27 *U. Chi. L. Rev.* 184 (1959). *The Almanac of Liberty* by Douglas was published (New

York, Doubleday & Company) in 1954. The paragraphs following the reference to the *Almanac* are essentially straight Douglas as reflected in the Countryman volume; these run to the reference to the April, 1964, antitrust decision, *United States* v. *First National Bank & Trust Co.*, No. 36, October term, 1963. The quotation from the clerk is from William Cohen, "Justice Douglas: A Law Clerk's View," 26 *U. Chi. L. Rev.* 6 (1958). The quotation beginning "Research on disease lags" is from the Douglas lectures published as *America Challenged* (Princeton, N.J., Princeton University Press, 1960). The 1963 election case is *Gray* v. *Sanders,* 372 U.S. 368, 83 Sup. Ct. 801, 9 L. Ed. 2d 821 (1963). The Manhattan Island congressional-districting case is *Wright* v. *Rockefeller,* 84 Sup. Ct. 603 (1964). The Florida case involving the National Association for the Advancement of Colored People is *Gibson* v. *Florida Legislative Investigation Committee,* 372 U.S. 539, 83 Sup. Ct. 889, 9 L. Ed. 2d 929 (1963).

CHAPTER FIVE   Mr. Justice Tom C. Clark

The steel-seizure case is *Youngstown Sheet & Tube Co.* v. *Sawyer,* 343 U.S. 579, 72 Sup. Ct. 863, 96 L. Ed. 1153 (1952). The 1963 prayer decision is *School District of Abington Tp., Pa.* v. *Schempp,* 374 U.S. 203, 83 Sup. Ct. 1560, 10 L. Ed. 2d 844 (1963). The three cases Clark argued in the Supreme Court while Attorney General were *United States* v. *United Mine Workers of America,* 330 U.S. 258, 67 Sup. Ct. 677, 91 L. Ed. 884 (1947); *United States* v. *State of California,* 332 U.S. 19, 67 Sup. Ct. 1658, 91 L. Ed. 1889 (1947); and *United States* v. *Paramount Pictures,* 334 U.S. 131, 68 Sup. Ct. 915, 92 L. Ed. 1260 (1948). The various references to the hearings on the Clark appointment come from *Hearings Before the Committee on the Judiciary, U.S. Senate, 81st Cong., 1st Sess., August 9, 10, 11, 1949, on the Nomination of Tom C. Clark.* The various newspaper and other quotations are contained therein.

189

The 1952 Oklahoma loyalty-oath case is *Weiman* v. *Updegraff*, 344 U.S. 183, 73 Sup. Ct. 215, 97 L. Ed. 216 (1952) ; and the case dealing with the claim of the privilege against self-incrimination in the course of a legislative investigation is *Slochower* v. *Board of Higher Ed. of City of N.Y.*, 350 U.S. 551, 76 Sup. Ct. 637, 100 L. Ed. 692 (1956). The 1964 opinion concerning the requirement that the race of candidates be included on the ballot is *Anderson* v. *Martin*, 375 U.S. 399, 84 Sup. Ct. 454, 11 L. Ed. 2d 430 (1964).

The case on documents in the possession of the prosecution is *Jencks* v. *United States*, 353 U.S. 657, 77 Sup. Ct. 1007, 1 L. Ed. 2d 1103 (1957). The decision upholding the right to counsel is *Gideon* v. *Wainwright*, 372 U.S. 335, 83 Sup. Ct. 792, 9 L. Ed. 799 (1963). The search-and-seizure case is *Mapp* v. *Ohio*, 367 U.S. 643, 81 Sup. Ct. 1684, 6 L. Ed. 2d 1081 (1961).

The three outstanding Clark opinions mentioned are, on searches and seizures, *Mapp*. v. *Ohio*, cited above; on the school-prayer cases, the Schempp case, also cited above; and on redistricting, *Baker* v. *Carr*, 369 U.S. 186, 82 Sup. Ct. 691, 7 L. Ed. 2d 663 (1962). The concluding quotation is from *This Week Magazine*, December 23, 1962.

CHAPTER SIX   Mr. Justice John Marshall Harlan

The quotation on Harlan's housing is taken from the December 4, 1954, issue of *The New Yorker* magazine. The details of Harlan's membership in the Atlantic Union Committee, the reference to the attitude of a head of the Antitrust Division, and the various matters taken up in connection with his confirmation come from *Hearings Before the Committee on the Judiciary, U.S. Senate, 84th Cong., 1st Sess., February 24, 25, 1955*. The Atlantic Union Committee materials are at p. 136, the antitrust reference at pp. 70–71, and the quotation on "The Wheel of Progress" is at pp. 124, 126. The further reference to the position of the senators on the Atlantic Union appears at p. 130. The reference to the "Order of the Acorn" appears at p. 99.

The quotation concerning Justice Whittaker appears at 40 *Tex. L. Rev.* 748 (1962).

The reference to dealing with the statute as it is found is from *United States* v. *Leslie Salt Co.,* 350 U.S. 383, 76 Sup. Ct. 416, 100 L. Ed. 441 (1956). The death sentence of Edwards is discussed in *Edwards* v. *People of the State of New York,* 76 Sup. Ct. 1058, 1 L. Ed. 2d 17 (1956). The Fifth Amendment reference is from *Noto* v. *United States,* 76 Sup. Ct. 255, 100 L. Ed. 1518 (1955). The Bucks County case is *United States* v. *Handy,* 351 U.S. 454, 76 Sup. Ct. 965, 100 L. Ed. 1331 (1956).

The loyalty-program case is *Cole* v. *Young,* 351 U.S. 536, 76 Sup. Ct. 861, 100 L. Ed. 1396 (1956). The second-string Communists case is *Yates* v. *United States,* 354 U.S. 298, 77 Sup. Ct. 1064, 1 L. Ed. 2d 1356 (1957). The second Communist case is *Scales* v. *United States,* 367 U.S. 203, 81 Sup. Ct. 1469, 6 L. Ed. 2d 782 (1961).

The statistics on voting are carried in an introductory article in each volume of the *Supreme Court Reporter.*

The Cuban sugar case is *Banco Nacional de Cuba* v. *Sabbatino,* 84 Sup. Ct. 923 (1964).

CHAPTER SEVEN   Mr. Justice William Brennan

The quotation from Max Freedman appeared in the *Manchester Guardian Weekly* on October 4, 1956. The statement on public understanding of the Court, made at Aspen, Colorado, was reported on August 30, 1963, in the *Washington Post* and on the AP wire. See also the *Aspen Times* of August 30, 1963. Much general information on the Justice is contained in an article in *Look* magazine, December 18, 1962, and in Jack Alexander's "The Justice from Jersey," *Saturday Evening Post,* September 28, 1957. The "Happy Irishman" story is from *Time* magazine, October 8, 1956. Miscellaneous biographical data was widely carried in the press at the time of his appointment, including *The New York Times,* September 30, 1956; the *Washing-*

ton Post on October 1, 1956; the *Hartford Times* of October 1, 1956; and the *New York Herald Tribune* of October 1, 1956.

The credit from Arthur T. Vanderbilt on the *New Jersey Manual of Pretrial Practice* is in the June, 1957, *American Bar Association Journal*. The disbarment case is *In re Herr*, 125 A.2d 706 (1956). The statements on Senator McCarthy were made on March 17, 1954, and December 3, 1954. The 1956 statement on the same subject is quoted in the *Washington Post* for September 30th of that year.

The appointment details were covered in a large number of newspapers on or about October 1, 1956. The Brennan family reaction is reflected in the *New York Herald Tribune* of October 1, 1956. The "nice guy" phrase comes from *The New York Times*, September 30, 1956. The *Des Moines Register* story is October 28, 1956, p. 13-G. The hearing details are reflected in the *Hearing Before the Committee on the Judiciary, United States Senate, 85th Cong., 1st Sess., February 26 and 27, 1957, on the Nomination of William Joseph Brennan, Jr.*

The case on the rights of Americans abroad is *Reid* v. *Covert*, 354 U.S. 1, 77 Sup. Ct. 1222, 1 L. Ed. 2d 1148 (1957). The search-and-seizure case is *Jencks* v. *United States*, 353 U.S. 657, 77 Sup. Ct. 1007, 1 L. Ed. 2d 1103 (1957). The apportionment case is *Baker* v. *Carr*, 369 U.S. 186, 82 Sup. Ct. 691, 7 L. Ed. 2d 663 (1962). The obscenity case is *Roth* v. *United States*, 354 U.S. 476, 77 Sup. Ct. 1304, 1 L. Ed. 2d 1498 (1957). The Du Pont–General Motors case is *United States* v. *E. I. du Pont de Nemours and Co.*, 366 U.S. 316, 81 Sup. Ct. 1243, 6 L. Ed. 2d 318 (1961). The Birmingham Police Commissioner's case is *New York Times Company* v. *L. B. Sullivan*, 84 Sup. Ct. 710 (1964). The 1963 dissent is *Wheeldin* v. *Wheeler*, 373 U.S. 647, 83 Sup. Ct. 1441, 10 L. Ed. 605 (1963). The 1963 school-prayer case is *School District of Abington Tp., Pa.* v. *Schempp*, 374 U.S. 203, 83 Sup. Ct. 1560, 10 L. Ed. 2d 844 (1963).

The quotation in conclusion is taken from the *Look* article cited above.

CHAPTER EIGHT   Mr. Justice Potter Stewart

General sources used on Justice Stewart include the Winter, 1960, *Yale Law Report* and the *Harvard Law Record* of October 29, 1959. Two interviews with the Justice also used are reported in *U.S. News & World Report*, December 10, 1962, and the *Cincinnati Post & Times Star*, June 8, 1963. The principal biographical article that has been used covering his pre-Supreme Court experience is Daniel M. Berman, "Mr. Justice Stewart: A Preliminary Appraisal," 28 *U. Cinc. L. Rev.* 401 (1959). The major review of his work on the Court of Appeals before his appointment to the Supreme Court that has been liberally used here is Professor J. Francis Paschal's "Mr. Justice Stewart on the Court of Appeals," 1959 *Duke L. J.* 325.

The segregation case before the Court of Appeals is *Clemons* v. *Board of Education of Hillsboro*, 228 F.2d 853 (6th Cir., 1956). The speedy-justice criminal case is *Henderson* v. *Bannan*, 256 F.2d 363 (6th Cir. 1958).

The important case decided before Stewart was confirmed was *Frank* v. *State of Maryland*, 359 U.S. 360, 79 Sup. Ct. 804, 3 L. Ed. 2d 877 (1959), and the newspaper comment was by Arthur Krock, *The New York Times*, May 7, 1959, as set forth in Senate Report 1893, 86th Cong. 2d Sess., August 22, 1960, on a proposed resolution by Senator Hart of Michigan that recess appointments should not normally be made. For discussion of the appointment on the floor of the Senate, see *Congressional Record*, May 5, 1959, Vol. 105, Part 6, pp. 7452–64.

The Louisiana kidnapping case is *Rideau* v. *State of Louisiana*, 373 U.S. 723, 83 Sup. Ct. 1417, 10 L. Ed. 2d 663 (1963). The New Mexico advertising case is *Head* v. *New Mexico Bd. of Exam. in Optometry*, 374 U.S. 424, 83 Sup. Ct. 1759, 10 L. Ed. 2d 983 (1963). The Nebraska–Missouri River case is *Durfee* v. *Duke*, 375 U.S. 106, 84 Sup. Ct. 242, 11 L. Ed. 2d 186 (1963).

The hotel search case is *Stoner* v. *State of California,* 84 Sup. Ct. 889 (1964).

The New York school-prayer case is *Engel* v. *Vitale,* 370 U.S. 421, 82 Sup. Ct. 1261, 8 L. Ed. 2d 601 (1962), and the later Pennsylvania case is *School District of Abington Tp., Pa.* v. *Schempp,* 374 U.S. 203, 83 Sup. Ct. 1560, 10 L. Ed. 2d 844 (1963).

Lady Chatterley's day in court came in *Kingsley International Pictures Corp.* v. *Regents of N.Y.U.,* 360 U.S. 684, 79 Sup. Ct. 1362, 3 L. Ed. 2d 1512 (1959).

Stewart's analysis of some of the problems of criminal defense were developed by him in an address to the Legal Aid Society of New York in February of 1960, reprinted in "The Legal Aid Brief Case," April, 1960. His remarks on the future of desegregation are contained in the *Cincinnati Post & Star* interview cited above.

CHAPTER NINE   Mr. Justice Byron R. White

An excellent article on White, used here, is Alfred Wright, "A Modest All-American Who Sits on the Highest Bench," 17 *Sports Illustrated* 84 (December 10, 1962).

The incidents involving the Freedom Riders in Alabama are reported in *The New York Times* for May 20, May 22, and May 27, 1961, these issues containing specific references to White, while all papers of that period contain general references to him. The quotation from President Kennedy on White's appointment appears, among many other places, in the *Sports Illustrated* article cited. So is the quotation concerning White's military experience.

On the appointment of judges, the quotations from White come from his remarks before the National Conference of Bar Presidents at Chicago, Illinois, on February 17, 1962, and from his remarks to the House of Delegates of the American Bar Association on February 19, 1962. Also used in this connection is the statement of Mr. Bernard Segal, Chairman of the Standing Committee on Federal Judiciary of the American Bar Association during the period of White's service as well as at other times, to the House of Delegates of the American Bar Association on February 19, 1962, and Mr. Segal's annual reports in 86 *Reports of American Bar Association* 503 (1961) and 87 *Reports of American Bar Association* 601 (1962).

The hearings on the White appointment are covered in *Hearings Before the Senate Committee on the Judiciary, 87th Cong., 2nd Sess., April 11, 1962, on the Nomination of Byron R. White.* The two White opinions of May 13, 1963, are *Gutierrez* v. *Waterman Steamship Corp.,* 373 U.S. 206, 83 Sup. Ct. 1185, 10 L. Ed. 2d 297 (1963), and *National Labor Relations Board* v. *Erie Resistor Corp.,* 373 U.S. 221, 83 Sup. Ct. 1139, 10 L. Ed. 2d 308 (1963). The dissent in the Cuban sugar case is in *Banco Nacional de Cuba* v. *Sabbatino,* 84 Sup. Ct. 923 (1964). The Washington criminal case is *Draper* v. *State of Washington,* 372 U.S. 487, 83 Sup. Ct. 774, 9 L. Ed. 2d 899 (1963).

The closing quotation from *The New Yorker* appears November 30, 1963, pp. 51–52.

CHAPTER TEN   Mr. Justice Arthur Goldberg

While Justice Goldberg has been the subject of intense public interest, with a large number of short news clips and sketches, the major publication concerning him is a Profile in *The New Yorker* for April 7 and 14, 1962. Much of the general information here was first found there.

The views of Judge John J. Parker on extrajudicial duties are contained in the *Handbook for Judges* of the American Judicature Society.

The Illinois Supreme Court decision early in Goldberg's career is *People* v. *Bruner,* 343 Ill. 146, 175 N.E. 400 (1931). The arbitration case referred to is *Textile Workers Union* v. *Lincoln Mills,* 353 U.S. 448, 77 Sup. Ct. 912, 1 L. Ed. 2d 972 (1957). The case on federal preemptions in labor disputes is *Amalgamated Ass'n. etc.* v. *Wisconsin*

Employment Rel. Bd., 340 U.S. 383, 71 Sup. Ct. 359, 95 L. Ed. 364 (1951). The first steel case referred to is *Youngstown Sheet & Tube Co.* v. *Sawyer,* 343 U.S. 579, 72 Sup. Ct. 863, 96 L. Ed. 1153 (1952). The second is *United Steel Workers* v. *United States,* 361 U.S. 39, 80 Sup. Ct. 1, 4 L. Ed. 2d 12 (1959).

The "activist" quotation is taken from the Newark, New Jersey, *Sunday Star Ledger,* November 3, 1963. The references to the "Goldberg Room" and the comparison with Secretary McNamara are taken from *The New Yorker* article cited above.

The appointment letter of President Kennedy is quoted in *The New York Times* for September 20, 1962. The other quotations relating to the appointment come largely from the *Hearings Before the Senate Committee on the Judiciary, 87th Cong., 2d Sess., September 11–13, 1962.*

Goldberg's opinion on alien reentry, which reviews the earlier cases mentioned, is *Rosenberg* v. *Fleuti,* 374 U.S. 449, 83 Sup. Ct. 1804, 10 L. Ed. 2d 1000 (1963). His later dissent on the related subject is *Mrvica* v. *Esperdy,* 84 Sup. Ct. 833 (1964). The opinion on American citizenship is *Kennedy* v. *Mendoza-Martinez,* 372 U.S. 144, 83 Sup. Ct. 554, 9 L. Ed. 2d 1013 (1963).

The comment on the Stewart opinion occurs in *Townsend* v. *Sain,* 372 U.S. 293, 83 Sup. Ct. 745, 9 L. Ed. 2d 770 (1963). The Potofsky quotation is taken from the hearings on the appointment.

Table of Cases Cited

Index

INDEX

200